You Know You're Past It When …

You Know You're Past It When …

Shelley Klein

Illustrations by
Louise Morgan

Michael O'Mara Books Limited

First published in 2008 by
Michael O'Mara Books Limited
9 Lion Yard
Tremadoc Road
London SW4 7NQ

ISBN: 978-1-84317-329-8
  3 5 7 9 10 8 6 4 2

Designed and typeset by K DESIGN, Somerset

Printed and bound in Great Britain by Clays Ltd, St Ives plc

www.mombooks.com

For all who are still young at heart.

Acknowledgements

I would like to thank the following people for their help, extremely useful suggestions and general support during the compilation of this book: Gillian Condon, Natasha McCormick, Mabel, Elsie and Sybil McCormick. Thanks also to Geoff Tibballs, and to Kate Gribble, whose editing of and general contribution to this collection were invaluable.

YOU KNOW YOU'RE PAST IT WHEN ...

- You can live without sex, but not without your glasses.

- You have all the time in the world to put your snapshots in photo albums, but you have no idea who the people in the photos are.

- Happy hour is a nap in the afternoon.

- Your children are beginning to look middle-aged.

- You keep more food than beer in the fridge.

- You're asleep, but others worry that you're dead.

- You and your teeth don't sleep together.

- Your ears are hairier than your head.

CUTTING-EDGE FASHION

Elizabeth K, a Dutch fashion designer, was very excited when she was given a once-in-a-lifetime opportunity to take part in a prestigious New York fashion show at the Guggenheim Museum.

She worked for weeks on end on her collection, perfecting her designs. Then, because she didn't trust anyone else to make them, she did all the sewing herself. Day after day she sat in her studio, creating stunning dresses and skirts, stitching feathers and sequins on to the clothes by hand until, come the night of the show, the models climbed into the garments. In order that there was no VPL (visible panty line), Elizabeth K insisted no underwear be worn.

As the music began, the models all started to parade down the catwalk, strutting their funky stuff. Suddenly, the audience began wolf-whistling and clapping. Elizabeth was pleased, but also a little disconcerted.

Then she realized what she'd done. In her desperation to get the collection finished on time, she'd forgotten to sew any linings into the garments. With the catwalk backlighting, *everything* was revealed. Needless to say, the show was a great success – although it took the models some time to appreciate exactly what it was that everyone was applauding.

DUFF

Most people know they're past it when their memories begin to fail them, which is something of which Lady Diana Cooper was all too aware.

'I have a horrible dislike of old age,' she once remarked. 'Everybody's dead – half, no, nearly all of one's contemporaries – and those that aren't are gaga. Someone rang the other day and said, "I want to invite you and Duff over for dinner." And I said, "But Duff's been dead for twenty-eight years."'

> 'They tell you that you'll lose your mind when you grow older. What they don't tell you is that you won't miss it very much.'
>
> MALCOLM COWLEY

BIG MISTAKE

Forgetting your passport when you're going on holiday is not a good idea, nor is leaving your bag on a bus, but one violinist took forgetfulness to real extremes recently when he left £180,000 worth of seventeenth-century Italian violin on a train luggage rack.

'I thought I couldn't possibly forget it,' he said. 'It was just one of those terrible moments when I realized, as the train was steaming off, that I had.'

BAD SEX

A middle-aged man was having an annual physical. As the doctor was listening to his heart with the stethoscope, the medic exclaimed, 'Oh, no!'

In a panic, the man asked the doctor what the problem was.

'Well,' said the physician, 'you have a bad heart murmur. Do you smoke?'

'No,' replied the man.

'Do you drink a lot?'

'No.'

'Do you have a vigorous sex life?'

'Yes, I do!'

'Well,' said the physician, 'I'm afraid with this heart murmur, you'll have to give up half your sex life.'

Looking confused, the man enquired, 'Which half? The looking or the thinking?'

NO TIME FOR LOITERING

One day in 1947, the author and journalist Wynford Vaughan Thomas was invited to accompany the South African prime minister, Jan Smuts, on his 'morning stroll' up Table Mountain.

Vaughan Thomas reached the top of the mountain some ten minutes after Smuts, who was by then in his seventies.

'Young man,' Smuts said, 'at my age, I haven't as much time as you for loitering.'

FORGET SOMETHING?

Often the first sign of ageing is when you start forgetting things, but a certain shoplifter took this to extremes one day when trying to make a quick getaway from a Dutch supermarket.

The forty-five-year-old thief, who stole a large packet of meat from a shop in the southern town of Kerkade, had run swiftly to his car, even pushing out of his way a supermarket employee who had tried to stop him by throwing himself across the car's bonnet.

However, the light-fingered gentleman had made one serious error: he'd forgotten his twelve-year-old son back in the supermarket. Police later arrested the man – having reunited him with the boy.

WHAT A SCHMUCK!

Husbands and wives often make each other feel as though they're past it, but nowhere is this more apparent than in the following joke, taken from *The Ultimate Book of Jewish Jokes*.

Sadie tells Maurice, 'You're a schmuck! You always were a schmuck and you always will be a schmuck! You look, act and dress like a schmuck! You'll be a schmuck until the day you die! And if they ran a worldwide competition for schmucks, you would be the world's second-biggest schmuck!'

'Why only second place?' Maurice asks.

'Because you're a schmuck!' Sadie screams.

WHICH WAY ARE YOU GOING?

Some people know they're past their prime when they forget where they've put their car keys, others when they forget where they've parked the car, but one woman caused mayhem in March 2008 when she drove for fifteen miles up the wrong side of the M65!

According to an article in *The Times*, the woman became confused when confronted with a 'new traffic configuration' at a roundabout. Police followed the car for seven junctions until they could bring her to a halt around Barrowfoot.

In mitigation, she explained, 'There was nowhere to turn around.'

GOOD NEWS AND BAD NEWS

The doctor led his patient into his office, sat her down, and said, 'I have some good news and some bad news.'

The woman said, 'Give me the good news.'

The doctor said, 'They're going to name a disease after you.'

BAD HAIR DAY

Two ladies were discussing the upcoming dance at the village hall.

'We're supposed to wear something that matches our husbands' hair, so I'm wearing black,' said Mrs Allan.

'Oh my,' said Mrs Pringle, 'I'd better not go.'

DÉJÀ VU?

Renowned for his absent-mindedness, the former publisher of the *New York Post*, J. David Stern, was once hurrying down the street when he bumped into an old friend, who invited him for lunch.

Stern agreed, although he asked if they could go to a nearby restaurant as he was already running late.

They entered the establishment and sat down at a table, but when it came to making an order, Stern couldn't understand why he didn't feel very hungry.

'I beg your pardon, sir,' said the waiter, 'but you just finished lunch five minutes ago.'

SENIOR-SAFETY CAP

In 2008, a man in his mid-fifties had to be rushed to hospital, having made his eye bleed while trying to open a bottle of pills.

He was attempting to unscrew the child-safety cap from a container of anti-inflammatory drugs, which he was taking for his arthritis, but he struggled so much that his hand flew backwards and punched him hard in the face.

To add insult to injury, the nurses at the hospital then enquired if it was his wife who had hit him and offered to alert a social worker. At that point, he knew he had to give up.

'If I didn't feel old before the incident,' he was quoted as saying, 'I did afterwards. Very, very old. Washed up, embarrassed, absolutely past it!'

THE UNDIPLOMATIC DIPLOMAT

Why is it, do you think, that the most undiplomatic of people often end up going into the diplomatic service?

This was certainly the case with Warren Austin, a US delegate to the United Nations, who was once asked to advise on the Middle East problem.

Forgetting to whom he was talking, or perhaps simply forgetting to engage his brain before opening his mouth, he was heard to advise both the Jewish and Arab delegates to 'sit down and settle their differences like Christians'.

I'M OUT

According to Owen Chadwick in his biography of Michael Ramsey, who was later to become Archbishop of Canterbury, one day Ramsey left his lodgings in Boston, Lincolnshire without his front door key.

After taking a short walk, he went back and rang his doorbell to gain entrance, but his landlady was so nervous of strangers that she called out to him through the letter box that she couldn't open the door because 'Mr Ramsey is out'.

'Never mind,' replied the absent-minded Ramsey. 'I'll return later.'

OH BERYL!

During a lunch at Buckingham Palace, award-winning novelist Beryl Bainbridge is reported to have run into difficulty due to the palace's strict no-smoking policy.

According to Fay Weldon, who was also present at the lunch, Bainbridge 'was telling this woman what a terribly boring party it was. Someone dragged her away. "You can't speak to the Queen like that!"

'"Oh dear," said Bainbridge. "I thought it was Vera Lynn."'

YOU KNOW YOU'RE PAST IT WHEN ...

- Your worst enemy is gravity.

- You talk about good grass and you're discussing someone's lawn.

- You have a party and your neighbours don't even realize.

- You receive more get-well cards than bills.

- You chase women, but can't remember why.

- People call at 9 p.m. and ask, 'Did I wake you?'

- Dialling long distance wears you out.

- You know what the word 'equity' means.

- You sink your teeth into a steak – and they stay there.

HEADLESS CHICKEN

When you start forgetting your lines, like actor Paul Bailey apparently did when he appeared at Stratford-upon-Avon in *Richard III*, you know you're getting on in life.

In the production, Christopher Plummer was playing the title role while Bailey took the part of Lovell, who during Act III has to appear on stage and say the line, 'Here is the head of that ignoble traitor, the dangerous and unsuspected Hastings.'

However, on the night in question, Bailey completely forgot his line and instead simply stared at Plummer for what seemed like ages.

Eventually, Plummer had to help him out by asking, 'Is that the head of that ignoble traitor, the dangerous and unsuspected Hastings?'

To which Bailey simply replied, 'Yes.'

TAKING THE BLAME

A farmer and his wife were standing outside their chicken coop, watching the chicks feed on grain, when the woman happily recalled that the next month would mark their silver wedding anniversary.

'Let's throw a party, Dave,' she suggested. 'Let's kill a chicken.'

The farmer scratched his grizzled head. 'Gee, Annie,' he finally answered, 'I don't see why the chicken should take the blame for something that happened twenty-five years back.'

A COUPLE OF OLD JOKES

In the excellent *2,500 Anecdotes for All Occasions*, edited by Edmund Fuller, there are many jokes about being past it, but the following two about forgetful professors are definitely my favourites.

1. 'That absent-minded Professor Schmaltz has left his umbrella again. He'd leave his head if it were loose,' observed the waiter.

    'That's true,' said the manager. 'I just heard him say he was going to Switzerland for his lungs.'

2. 'Did you see this?' the professor's wife asked him as he arrived home. 'There's a report in the paper of your death.'

    'Dear me,' replied her husband. 'We must remember to send a wreath.'

LOWER, LOWER

A frustrated man goes to see his GP.

'Doc, I want my sex drive lowered.'

'Now, now,' answered the doctor, 'you're getting on a bit these days. Don't you think your libido is all in your head?'

'You're damned right it is!' replied the man. 'That's why I want it lowered!'

IN A MUDDLE

The TV broadcaster Hugh Scully must know all about feeling past it, for at the end of a BBC television interview with Liza Minelli on the programme *Nationwide*, he apparently ended the Q-and-A session by saying, 'Thank you, Judy Garland.'

Luckily, Minelli was on good form that day and saved the moment by replying, 'I'll tell Liza.'

GOING DOWN IN FLAMES

A Polish man managed to destroy an entire apartment block while trying to remove troublesome ants from a ventilation shaft. He poured gallons of insecticide down the shaft, but when that had no obvious effect, he threw in a burning towel for good measure. The resulting explosion reduced the building to rubble, but – amazingly – nobody was injured.

> 'A medical report states that the human male is physically capable of enjoying sex up to and even beyond the age of eighty. Not as a participant, of course.'
>
> DENIS NORDEN

SOUR CREAM

You definitely know you're past it when your children point out your shortcomings. Take, for example, the following anecdote from *Pass the Port* by Christian Brann.

'While watching her mother put some face cream on, a little girl was overheard to ask: "Mummy, is that the cream they show on the television that makes you beautiful?"

'The mother replied that it was, only for her daughter to say, "It doesn't work very well, does it?"'

Ouch!

HOUSEWORK HOSTAGE

It's a sure sign you're past your prime when your ex-boyfriend kidnaps you so that you can do his housework. That's exactly what happened to a forty-something woman in Genoa, Italy, who was dragged out of a pub by her former lover, pushed into a car and taken back to his home, where he forced her to iron his clothes and wash dishes.

SWAPSIES

A rather mature man and woman got married. After the wedding, the couple went to a hotel. On the first night, the groom went to the bathroom and was in there for ages.

'What's taking you so long?' asked the bride.

'I'm brushing my teeth,' replied the groom.

'It doesn't take that long to brush your teeth,' said the bride.

'I'm brushing yours too,' answered the groom.

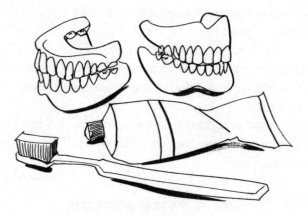

HOT FLUSH

It was a hot sunny day as Caroline left the plumber's yard, and several young workmen were sitting around shirtless. To match the weather, Caroline herself was wearing a shorter skirt than usual, revealing a shapely pair of legs for someone in her late forties. She was aware of the workmen as she walked to her car, but was taken completely by surprise when she heard a male voice call out, 'Can I have your phone number?'

Caroline blushed slightly. What would her husband say? It was years since she had been propositioned and she was flattered by the attention. But she continued walking towards her car, albeit with an extra wiggle of her bottom.

Then the shout came again: 'Please can I have your phone number?'

Her mind was now racing to guess which of the workmen was her admirer; was it the Brad Pitt lookalike with the tanned body or the dark-haired one with the tattoos? Either way, it had made her day.

Still determined not to turn around, she self-consciously adjusted the hem of her skirt before delving into her bag for her car keys. She was just about to unlock the car when the voice shouted for a third time, more urgently than before: 'Please can I have your phone number?'

It was time for the ice maiden to melt: to hell with the boring husband and the three kids; she wanted some excitement in her life and turned to see which young stud found her irresistible.

The workmen were indeed staring at her, as was a bald-headed man in his sixties, breathlessly clutching a piece of paper.

'Please can I have your phone number, Mrs McLean,' he shouted, 'or I won't be able to let you know when we can deliver your new toilet cistern.'

WAY TO GO

Death is one of life's certainties and, for those of a particular age, it holds something of a peculiar fascination. As we grow older, we start to wonder, rather morbidly, just how we might leave this earth.

So, when little Danny's pet hamster died, and a kindly neighbour helped him to bury it in the garden, death was not far from the elderly neighbour's thoughts.

Placing his hand on the boy's shoulder, the man explained carefully that death comes to all creatures, man and beast, and that the hamster had lived a full life and received a proper burial, just as it should be.

'So, little boy, how would you like to die?' queried the man.

Danny pondered the question solemnly, and then replied: 'I want to die sleeping like my grandfather, not screaming like the passengers in the car.'

TOO OLD TO REMEMBER

Two clergymen were in London to attend a week's synod at Church House. They were having tea and biscuits in front of the fire, discussing how they were going to deal with the subject of the next day's conference. It was a difficult topic for clergymen – premarital sex.

'For instance,' said one of them, 'I never slept with my wife before I married her. Did you?'

'I can't remember,' said the other. 'What was her maiden name?'

AMAZING

One day, the octogenarian Austrian economist Ludwig von Mises was asked how he felt getting up each morning.

His reply?

'Amazed!'

RAISING THE DEAD

A middle-aged couple were watching a healing service on a cable channel. The evangelist called to all who wanted to be healed to go to their television set, place one hand on the TV and the other hand on the body part where they needed treatment.

The wife got up and walked to the television, then placed her right hand on the set and her left hand on her arthritic shoulder that was causing her great pain. Then the husband got up, went to the TV, placed his right hand on the set and his left hand on his crotch.

Hi missus scowled at him and said, 'I guess you just don't get it. The purpose of doing this is to heal the sick, not raise the dead.'

HOW VERY RUDE!

A certain rather haggard-looking cellist certainly knew he was well past his prime when, one night, it is said that US comedian Fred Allen turned up at the vaudeville house at which he was playing and shouted down to him: 'How much would you charge to haunt a house?'

CRUELTY TO ANIMALS

The Greek poet Aeschylus certainly knew the dangers of growing old, for it is said that his death came about when an eagle, who had captured a tortoise and needed a stone on which to break open the poor creature's shell, mistook Aeschylus's bald head for a rock ... and dropped the tortoise on it!

THE IMPORTANCE OF BEING IMPORTANT

The following extract from D. J. Enright's *Play Resumed* sums up perfectly that moment when you definitely know you are past it.

> The contents of this envelope are important and require your immediate attention. To begin with, opening the envelope is a major undertaking, and wouldn't be easy if you were in full possession of your fingers. And then, though you labour to make them so, the contents are not in the least important to you, nor you to them. Why is everything *important* these days? Because so many things are of no consequence.

A. E. MATTHEWS

For an actor, who has to learn hundreds of lines, growing old is particularly difficult and nowhere is this better illustrated than in the case of A. E. Matthews, who is once said to have reassured the director of the play he was working on: 'I know you think I'm not going to learn my lines, but I promise you that even if we had to open next Monday, I would be all right.'

'But Matty,' replied the director, 'we *do* open next Monday!'

GOOD PUT-DOWN

You know for sure you're entering your golden years when everyone around you starts to look (and generally is) younger than you. Policemen seem to be about fifteen years old and doctors about twelve, so imagine the Hollywood director Billy Wilder's consternation when he was summoned to the studio by the 'movie brat' who had taken over as head.

'Great to meet you at last, Billy,' the youngster is supposed to have said. 'Hope you'll come on the team. Believe we can make you some very interesting offers. Now, Billy, tell me – what have you done?'

Wilder is said to have paused a second and then replied politely: 'After you ...'

PRESENCE OF OLD AGE

A grandmother was giving directions to her grandson, who was coming to visit her with his wife and kids.

'You come to the front door of the apartment block. I am in apartment 16A. There is a big panel at the door. With your elbow, push button 16A. I will buzz you in. Come inside, the elevator is on the right. Get in, and with your elbow hit 16. When you get out, I am on the left. With your elbow, hit my doorbell.'

'Grandma, that sounds easy,' replied the grandson, 'but I don't understand why I'm hitting all these buttons with my elbow.'

To which she answered, 'You're coming empty-handed?'

YOU KNOW YOU'RE PAST IT WHEN ...

- It takes longer to rest than it did to get tired.

- You no longer think of speed limits as a challenge.

- If you have to allow six weeks for an order, you think twice about placing it.

- Your knees buckle, but your belt won't.

- You know your doctor's phone number, but you can't remember your children's.

- Your idea of a night out is sitting on the patio.

- You know the difference between a gastroenterologist, oncologist and phlebotomist.

- There's no question in your mind that there's no question in your mind.

ON RETIREMENT

No one talks about retirement quite like the curmudgeonly TV sitcom character Victor Meldrew from *One Foot in the Grave*, written by David Renwick.

'I'm retired,' Meldrew said. 'I'm now officially a lower form of life than a Duracell battery. I've been replaced by a box. It's standard procedure apparently for a man of my age. The next stage is to stick you inside one.'

BOILING POINT

Even distinguished scientists like Sir Isaac Newton can be prone to lapses of memory, as the following story attests.

One day, a kitchen maid in Sir Isaac's house found the great man standing in front of a large pot of boiling water. He looked down at his hand, in which he was holding an egg, then glanced at the pot: at the bottom of which lay his watch.

WHAT A BOTHER

French actor Maurice Chevalier and US comedian Phil Silvers were chatting backstage one evening during a show, when a group of lovely young women passed by.

Chevalier sighed longingly. 'Ah,' he remarked, 'if only I were twenty years older.'

'Don't you mean twenty years younger?' Silvers asked.

'No, if I were twenty years older,' Chevalier replied, 'these girls would not bother me the way they do!'

WHAT A DOPE

A forty-five-year-old Chinese farmer accidentally knocked himself out for eleven hours while he was supposed to be anaesthetizing deer. After administering a tranquilizing shot to a deer, Mr Liu noticed anaesthetic dripping from the needle and, while using his hand to wipe it, somehow contrived to inject himself.

SIMPLE LOGIC

Two ladies sat on a bench, talking.

One said to the other, 'Good heavens! Who did your hair? It looks like a wig!'

The second lady replied, 'It is a wig.'

'Really?' pondered the first woman. 'You could never tell!'

WHO IS THAT MAN?

For many years, Groucho Marx and the bestselling author Sidney Sheldon were close Hollywood friends and neighbours. In his eighties, Groucho was in the habit of popping round to visit Sheldon and his wife every afternoon for a little snack of an apple and a chunk of cheese.

'It became such a ritual,' Sheldon recalled, 'that my wife and I looked forward to it every day.'

However, when the Sheldons decided to rent out their Hollywood mansion and move to Rome, confusion ensued.

One morning, Sidney received a letter from his tenant saying: 'We love the house, but there is one strange thing. Every afternoon, there is a little old man, between eighty-five and ninety, who knocks at our door and asks for some cheese and an apple. He's too well dressed for a tramp. Can you tell us who he is?'

NO REPEATS

An anxious senior citizen telephoned her doctor. 'Is it accurate to say,' she demanded, 'that the pills you have prescribed me must be taken till the very end of my days?'

'Yes, I'm afraid so,' her GP said firmly.

There was a pause, before the lady responded, 'I'm wondering, then, just how serious my condition is, because this prescription is marked "no repeats"?'

BANANAS!

You definitely know you're past it when your husband acts like this …

'As I stripped off my sweatshirt at the breakfast table one warm morning, my T-shirt started to come off too. My husband let out a low whistle. I took it as a compliment – until he said, from behind his newspaper, 'Can you believe the price of bananas?'

So wrote Beatrice Roche in *Reader's Digest*.

PRENUPTIALS

A couple in their sixties were about to get married.

She said, 'I want to keep my house.'

He said, 'That's okay with me.'

She said, 'And I want to keep my Mercedes.'

He said, 'That's fine with me too.'

She said, 'And I want to have sex six times a week.'

He said, 'That's fine with me. Put me down for Thursdays.'

MIRACULOUS CURES

A doctor, who was renowned for his exceptional results in treating arthritis, had a waiting room chock-full of patients.

A lady, whose back was curved into a most painful-looking arc, shuffled in slowly, bent double, relying heavily on her wooden stick. All who saw her pitied her.

When her name was called, she hobbled into the consultant's office. Incredibly, within five minutes, she emerged a new woman, walking completely upright with her head held high.

A man in the waiting room, who had seen all this, rushed up to the revived patient and declared, 'My God, it's a miracle! I saw it with my own eyes. You walked in here with the worst arthritis I've ever seen and now you're strolling out with a totally straight back! What on earth did the doctor do?'

'He gave me a longer cane,' she replied.

THE OLDER YOU GROW,
THE MORE WILY YOU GET

A hotshot New York lawyer in his twenties went grouse shooting in rural Tennessee. He shot and killed a bird, but it fell into a farmer's field on the other side of a fence. As the lawyer climbed over the fence, the farmer drove up on his tractor and asked him what he was doing.

The lawyer replied, 'I shot a grouse and it fell into this field, and now I'm going to pick it up.'

The farmer, drawing on his years of experience, replied, 'This is my property, and you are not coming over here.'

The lawyer said, 'I am one of the best attorneys in the US and if you don't let me get that game bird, I'll sue you and take everything you own.'

The farmer grinned and said, 'Apparently, you don't know how we do things here in Tennessee. We settle small disagreements like this with the Tennessee Three-Kick Rule.'

'What is the Tennessee Three-Kick Rule?' asked the lawyer.

The farmer replied, 'Well, first I kick you three times and then you kick me three times, and so on, back and forth, until someone gives up.'

The attorney thought about the proposed contest and decided that he could easily take the old man down, so he agreed that the contest should go ahead.

The farmer slowly climbed down from the tractor and walked up to the city boy. His first kick planted the toe of his heavy boot into the lawyer's groin and dropped him to his knees. His second kick nearly broke the man's nose. The barrister was flat on his belly when the farmer's third kick to a kidney nearly caused him to quit.

However, he summoned every bit of his will and managed to get to his feet and said, 'OK, enough! Now it's my turn.'

The old farmer smiled and said, 'No, I give up, you can have the grouse.'

YOU'RE NEXT!

Juliet Walsh, aged seventy-six, never tired of going to weddings, during which her favourite pastime was nudging all the twenty-year-olds and telling them, 'You're next.'

But Juliet soon stopped doing this when someone said the exact same thing to her – only this time, she was at a funeral!

DEAR OLD HUGH

Very few octogenarians have an active sex life. (Or do they?) Take, for example, the following report, reproduced in *Old Git Wit*, which seems to suggest that even Hugh Hefner might sadly be past it.

'Holly Madison, twenty-seven, has got engaged to Hugh Hefner, eighty. Asked what the founder of *Playboy* likes best in bed, Holly said, "The guard rail."'

INDECENT PROPOSAL

Three magistrates were trying a case of indecent assault. It was a sweltering morning and the courtroom was very hot.

On the chairwoman's right was a conscientious schoolteacher, while on her left was a retired admiral with a very grey beard. As frequently happens when you're getting on in life, he began to nod off and was soon fast asleep as the chairwoman asked the young woman in the witness box to write down what the accused man had said to her.

The girl wrote something down on a slip of paper, which was handed up to the chairwoman, who read it and then nudged the sleeping admiral to wake him. He gave a snort and woke up to find the following note being passed to him: 'I'm feeling really horny. What about coming back to my place for a quick one?'

He read it with horror and hastily handed it back to the chairwoman, whispering, 'Madam, control yourself. You must be out of your mind!'

'Have you not a moist eye, a dry hand, a yellow cheek, a white beard, a decreasing leg, an increasing belly? Is not your voice broken, your wind short, your chin double, your wit single, and every part about blasted with antiquity?'

WILLIAM SHAKESPEARE, *Henry IV, Part II*

BEATING FAST

Towards the end of her life, the actress Sarah Bernhardt lived in a top-floor apartment in Paris. One day, a fan of hers paid her a call, but became very out of breath having climbed up innumerable steps to get there.

'*Madame*,' he said, 'why do you live so high up?'

'My dear friend,' Bernhardt replied, 'it is the only way I can still make the hearts of men beat faster.'

GETTING HEALTHIER

Two guys were playing poker, talking, when the subject turned to getting older. The first guy said, 'Women have all the luck when it comes to growing old.'

'What do you mean?' asked the second guy.

'Well,' replied the first, 'I can't recall the last time I was able to get it up in bed, but my wife is healthier than ever.'

'Healthier? How do you mean?' his buddy wondered aloud.

'Years ago, when we were younger, every night before bed she'd get these terrible headaches,' his friend replied. 'But now that we're older, she hasn't had a headache in years.'

BARN CONVERSION

Similarly silly is the anecdote about the late, great Edith Evans, who on hearing that some people 'were living in Barnes' is supposed to have retorted, 'What? Couldn't they afford a house?'

YOU KNOW YOU'RE PAST IT WHEN ...

- You're on the floor cleaning or playing with the kids when the phone rings, and it's just easier to crawl to the phone than to get up and walk there.

- Your friends compliment you on your new alligator shoes ... but you're barefoot.

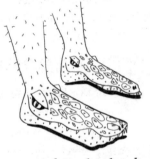

- You're given one of those books about the 'joys of ageing' as a present [such as this one] – Garrison Keillor.

- You turn out the light for economic reasons instead of romantic ones. – Herbert J. Karet

- Your doctor doesn't give you X-rays any more, but just holds you up to the light.

- You tell your friends you're having an affair and they ask, 'Are you having it catered?'

- A sexy babe catches your fancy – and your pacemaker opens the garage door nearest you.

- You're young at heart, but a lot older in other places.

IT'S EASY TO FORGET WHAT WE'VE FORGOTTEN

Forgetfulness is definitely one of the first signs of being past it, as the following anecdote, which first appeared in *Conversation, Please* by Loren Carroll, reveals.

A young lady who had called in on Agnes Repplier (an American writer and essayist) got ready to go, put on her hat and coat, put her hands in her muff, took them out, picked up a parcel, laid it down, shifted from one foot to another and then said, 'There was something I meant to say, but I've forgotten.'

'Perhaps, my dear,' Miss Repplier replied, 'it was goodbye.'

SILENCE IS GOLDEN

A couple go to Holy Communion one Sunday. Halfway through the service, the wife leans over and whispers in her husband's ear, 'I've just let out a silent fart. What should I do?'

The husband replies, 'Put a new battery in your hearing aid.'

Claudia: You know what the problem with getting old is, Henry?

Henry: No, what's the problem?

Claudia: What problem?

DECAYED TENEMENTS

In 1826, a former president of the United States, John Adams, suffered a bad stroke and passed away.

Describing his last meeting with Adams, his friend Daniel Webster said: 'Someone, a friend of his, came in and made particular enquiry of his health. Adams answered, "I inhabit a weak, frail, decayed tenement battered by the winds and broken in upon by the storms, and, from all I can learn, the landlord does not intend to repair!"'

HEAVEN'S WAITING ROOM

Journalist Gareth McLean obviously knew all the signs of being past it when he described the moment he realized he was ' ... surrounded by men in tartan trousers and bifocals and women whose last orgasm coincided with the Suez crisis. It was like being in the waiting room for heaven.'

FROM SHOW-BIZ TO NO-BIZ

No industry is more cruel to those no longer in the flush of youth than that of show business. As the acid-tongued Cher observed, 'In this business it takes time to be really good – and by that time, you're obsolete.'

GETTING YOUR OWN BACK

A middle-aged woman is in her birthday suit, trampolining enthusiastically on her bed, giggling and humming with wild abandon. Her husband walks into the room and sees her. He watches her a while, then remarks, 'You look absurd! What on earth do you think you're doing?'

She announces, 'I just had a medical exam and my doctor says I have the breasts of an eighteen-year-old.' She starts throwing herself about the bed again, trilling songs for all she's worth.

He snorts, 'Yeah, right. And what did he say about your ass?'

'Your name never came up,' she retorts.

RECOGNIZE HIM?

You know you're past it when people speak only well of you …

A gentleman had died. A wonderful funeral was taking place, during which the preacher talked at length of the good traits of the deceased. The preacher went on about 'what an honest man' and 'what a loving husband and kind father' he was.

Finally, the widow leaned over and whispered to her youngest child, 'Go up there and take a look in the coffin. See if that's your father in there.'

AGE-ACTIVATED ATTENTION DEFICIT DISORDER

As acronyms go, A. A. A. D. D. is one of those conditions that anyone who is past it must know only too well.

Browsers of the Internet (assuming, of course, that you're not already past it to the extent that such technological facilities are beyond your comprehension) may already be familiar with its symptoms, as countless websites list its collected traits. This is how it manifests itself.

You decide to water your garden.

As you turn on the hose in the driveway, you look over at your car and decide it needs washing.

As you start walking towards the garage for the cleaning miscellanea, you notice that there is mail on the porch table that you brought up from the letterbox earlier.

You decide to go through the mail before you wash the car.

You lay your car keys down on the table, put the junk mail in the rubbish bin under the table … and notice that the bin is full.

So you decide to put the bills back on the table and take out the rubbish – but then you think that since you're going to be near the postbox when you take out the bin bags, you may as well pay the bills first.

You take your chequebook off the table and see that there is only one cheque left. Your extra cheques are in your desk drawer in the study, so you go inside the house to your desk, where you find the can of Sprite that you had been drinking earlier.

You're going to look for your cheques, but first you need to put the Sprite to one side, so that you don't accidentally knock it over. You notice that the Sprite is getting warm so you decide that you should put it in the refrigerator to keep it cool.

As you head towards the kitchen with the Sprite, a vase of flowers on the counter catches your eye: they need to be watered.

You place the Sprite down on the work surface – and you discover your reading glasses, for which you've been searching all morning.

You decide you better put them back on your desk in their rightful place, but first you're going to water the flowers.

You set the glasses back down on the worktop, fill a container with water – then, suddenly, you spot the TV remote. Someone has left it on the kitchen table.

You realize that tonight when you go to watch TV, you will be looking for the remote, but you know you won't remember that it's on the kitchen table, so you decide to put it back in the lounge where it belongs. First, though, you'll water the flowers.

You pour some water in the vase, but quite a bit of it spills on the floor. So you set the remote back down on the table, get some towels and wipe up the mess.

Then you head down the hall, trying to remember what you were planning to do next.

At the end of the day:

- The car isn't washed.

- The bills aren't paid.

- The bin is overflowing.

- There is a warm can of Sprite sitting on the work surface.

- The flowers don't have enough water.

- There is still only one cheque in your chequebook.

- You can't find the remote.

- You can't locate your glasses ... and you don't remember what you did with the car keys.

Then, when you try to figure out why nothing got done today, you're really baffled, because you know you were busy all day long, and you're really tired. You realize this is a serious problem, so you make a mental note to get some help for it (which is, of course, not worth the paper it's written on). First, you see, you'll check your emails.

Afterword: you just remembered, you left the water running …

YOU KNOW YOU'RE PAST IT WHEN …

- Your other half says, 'Let's go upstairs and make love,' and you answer, 'Darling, I can't do both!'

- You start getting symptoms in the places you used to get urges. – Denis Norden

- Going braless pulls all the wrinkles out of your face.

- Your idea of a workout is getting into your bra every morning.

- It takes two tries to get up from the couch.

- You have two pairs of spectacles, one of which you use to locate the other.

- Your joints are more accurate than the National Weather Service.

QUESTION: How do you make four old ladies say 'F**k'?
ANSWER: Get a fifth old lady to shout 'Bingo!'

MORE HASTE, LESS SPEED

Janie was in a hurry to get to the bank before it closed. Trotting briskly to her car, she rummaged in her handbag for her keys, but couldn't find them anywhere. Realizing that her bag was already open, she figured that they must have fallen out and rolled under the car.

So, she got down on her hands and knees and crawled beneath the vehicle, contorting her body and stretching her fingers into the darkest recesses. Unable to feel the presence of the elusive keys, she decided to back out – only to discover that she was wedged fast beneath the axle.

No matter how much she tried to twist and turn, her body wouldn't move. She called out for help, but no one heard. All manner of thoughts passed through her mind: 'What persuaded me to climb under the car? Why did I have that extra slice of apple pie last week?'

She lay there for two whole days until a neighbour, concerned at not having seen her, investigated a weak banging sound from under the car and found the stricken Janie. Within half an hour, firefighters had pulled her free and discovered her car keys ... in the car door.

TOO OLD TO CARE

On being sent an invitation by a leading society hostess to the effect that she would be 'at home' that day, a curmudgeonly George Bernard Shaw is said to have replied, 'So will G. Bernard Shaw.'

OBSERVATIONS ON OLD AGE

In the TV show *3rd Rock from the Sun*, written by Andy Cowan, the characters provide these amusing insights into ageing:

Mary: When men get grey hair, they look distinguished. When women get grey hair, they look old.
Dick: When women get breasts, they look sexy. When men get breasts, they look old.

CONFUSED?

One day at the village Post Office, the woman behind the counter watched as the local doctor, who was then in his seventies and a little forgetful, carefully tried to write out a cheque to cover his electricity bill.

But the doctor looked a little frustrated, not to mention puzzled.

The woman behind the counter asked the doctor what was wrong. 'Perhaps I can help?' she suggested.

'Oh, I doubt it,' replied the doctor, looking down at his hand, in which lay a rectal thermometer. 'I was just trying to remember where I last left my pen.'

THE ATTENDANT

According to a tale related by journalist Walter Kiernan, a customer in a department store in Denmark walked into the ladies' toilets one day, only to be stared at in a very unfriendly manner by the attendant when she didn't leave a tip. The woman consequently complained to the management, who decided to do a check on the toilet attendant.

It transpired that she wasn't one of the store's employees at all, but a woman who had wandered into the restrooms a year previously and sat down to do a bit of knitting. Mistaking her for the attendant, customers began leaving her tips. So the woman had returned to the store every day, bringing her knitting with her.

PAST-IT POLITICIANS

American politicians have never been known for their intellect; in fact, quite a few of them have been in office while dangerously past it.

Senator Bob Dole was notorious for his lapses of memory, particularly when giving speeches. One day, for example, he was trying to explain to an interviewer the problems politicians faced keeping their private lives private.

'You read what Disraeli had to say,' Dole said, and then paused for quite a time. 'I don't remember what he said. He said something.' Another long pause, then: 'He's no longer with us.'

PLAIN TRUTH

Upon retiring, a woman decided to fulfill her lifelong dream and live abroad. As part of her preparations, she visited her doctor to pick up her medical records. The doctor asked her how she was doing, so with a sigh she reported a litany of symptoms – this aches, that's stiff, I'm not as quick as I used to be, and so on.

He responded with, 'Mrs Dickson, you have to expect things to start deteriorating. After all, who wants to live to a hundred?'

Mrs Dickson looked him straight in the eye and replied, 'Anyone who's ninety-nine.'

HOW LONG AGO WAS IT?

A minister decided to do something a little off the wall at his weekly sermon. He said to his parishioners, 'Today, in church, I am going to say a single word. And whichever single word I say, I want you to sing whichever hymn comes to your mind. And thus we will be united in thought, in worship and in life.'

The pastor shouted out 'Beautiful.'

Immediately, the congregation started singing, in unison, 'All Things Bright and Beautiful'.

The pastor hollered out 'Grace.'

The congregation chorused 'Amazing Grace.'

The pastor yelled, 'Dance!'

The congregation sang 'Lord of the Dance'.

The pastor said, 'Sex.'

The congregation fell into total silence.

Everyone was in shock. They all began to look around at each other nervously, afraid to say anything.

Then, from the back of the church, in a high, reed-thin voice, a weary middle-aged woman began to sing 'Precious Memories'.

EVERYTHING'S PEACHY

Alex was making love to his wife when suddenly, to his immense joy, Claire let out a short cry of pleasure.

'My goodness, darling!' he exclaimed. 'What happened?'

'It's amazing,' replied Claire. 'I finally decided that those cushions would look much better in peach.'

EXERCISE IS BAD FOR YOU

Exercise can be very bad for you at any age, but the older you get, the worse it can become. Australian author Clive James knows this only too well:

'Joggers are people who really believe that they can recapture their youth by taking exercise. The brutal facts suggest that unless you have never lost your youth, and have been taking exercise all the time, then trying to get fit will kill you as surely as a horse-kick to the heart.'

'My nan, she gets things mixed up, bless her. She gets the telephone mixed up with the hairdryer. You might have seen her around – wet hair, chapped lips.'

HARRY HILL

SIR JOHN GIELGUD

One evening, the inimitable Sir John Gielgud was in his dressing room, having just come off stage, when a man entered the room to congratulate him on his performance.

'How pleased I am to meet you,' exclaimed Sir John, who recognized the man's face. 'I used to know your son, we were at school together.'

'I don't have a son,' replied the man somewhat crossly. '*I* was the one who was at school with you.'

MURDER MOST TIRESOME

Growing old can mean growing tedious, though the worst affected will remain convinced of their sparkling wit and bonhomie.

American foreign correspondent Frank Sparks once attended a charity function at an exclusive Park Avenue address, where he found himself unfortunately seated next to an exceedingly dull criminologist.

After listening to this man's tiresome nonsense for about half an hour, Sparks made his excuses, got up and slipped into the next room, where he bumped into the event's organizer.

'He's a bit on the boring side, isn't he?' apologized the host. Sparks nodded. 'But he's got one of the finest minds in the city,' the party-giver continued. 'They tell me he's discovered how to commit the perfect crime.'

'I know,' hissed Sparks, 'he almost bored me to death too.'

HOME SWEET HOME?

You certainly know you're past it when you find yourself living in a retirement home – past it, at least, as far as your family is concerned, as this extract from TV show *Frasier* cold-heartedly demonstrates: 'Ah, the brochure for Dad's retirement home: "Golden Acres. We care so you don't have to."'

And how about this observation on the subject from Dame Edna Everage?

'My mother's suffering from advanced old-timer's disease so we've put her in a maximum-security Twilight Home for the Bewildered. Her accommodation is in the Sylvia Plath Suite. Other wards include the Virginia Woolf Incontinence Wing, the Diane Arbus X-Ray Unit, and the Zelda Fitzgerald Fire Escape.'

BACK FROM THE DEAD

There can be no greater sign that you're past it than when your own acquaintances think you're dead. Take, for instance, the following story, which involves three formidable ladies.

One day, in the actress Katherine Cornell's dressing room, Mrs Leslie Carter and Mrs Patrick Campbell greeted one another.

'I'm very honoured,' said Mrs Campbell. She took hold of Mrs Carter's hand and shook it, before turning to Katherine Cornell and, in a very loud voice, confided, 'I thought she was dead.'

YOU KNOW YOU'RE PAST IT WHEN ...

- Your idea of weight lifting is standing up.

- 'An all-nighter' means not getting up to use the bathroom.

- You look for your glasses for an hour ... and then find that they were on top of your head all the time.

- You can spell.

- You're more attractive standing on your head.

- Your wife believes your excuses for getting home late. – Basil Ransome-Davies

- The pharmacist has become your new best friend.

JAMES DUFFY AND FRED SWEENEY

There's forgetful and then there's *really* forgetful, as illustrated by the following anecdote.

A famous vaudeville act by the name of Sweeney and Duffy were booked in at a theatre. During the show, though Sweeney was on stage, no one could find Duffy. Finally, the stage manager found the AWOL actor having a Turkish bath around the corner from the theatre.

'For God's sake, Duffy, what are you doing here?' the stage manager yelled. 'You are on now!'

'I am?' replied an unruffled Duffy. 'How am I doing?'

ALMOST

Bernie had worked in the biscuit factory all his life, never finding the time to get married. Then, one sunny morning, a beautiful eighteen-year-old girl walked on to the shop floor and it was love at first sight.

Within a month, Bernie and Kate were married and on the way to California for their honeymoon.

'So how was it?' asked Martin, Bernie's colleague, on the couple's return.

'Oh, just wonderful,' replied a dewy-eyed Bernie. 'The sun, the surf ... and we made love almost every night. We –'

'Just a minute,' interrupted Martin. 'Forgive me for asking, but you made love almost every night – at your age?'

'Oh yes,' said Bernie, 'We almost made love Saturday, we almost made love Sunday ...'

NEW TRICKS, OLD DOGS

During an appearance on Conan O'Brien's TV show in August 2002, American comedian Tracy Morgan revealed how all of his friends were trying to become rap artists, including his forty-one-year-old brother.

'What's *he* rapping about?' Conan quickly joked. 'Lower back pain?'

SEAT, SIR?

The older one grows, the more one needs to sit down, as comic George Burns knew only too well.

Even in his golden years, he was still to be found performing two-hour shows. However, he explained, 'I do ten minutes standing up and fifty minutes sitting in a chair.'

LOOKING GOOD

Sheila is standing in front of her full-length mirror, taking a long, hard look at herself.

'You know, Steve,' she remarks. 'I stare into this mirror and I see an ancient creature. My face is all creased and tired, my skin is wrinkled, and my eyes have more bags than Paris Hilton on a transatlantic flight. My arms and legs are as flabby as jelly, and my bottom looks like several deflated, popped balloons. Observe my boobs – they droop so much that they hang to my waist. My body has just gone to pot.'

She turns to face her husband and says, 'Dear, please tell me just one good thing about my body so that I can feel a bit better about myself.'

Steve studies Sheila critically for a moment and then says in a gentle, thoughtful voice, 'Well, there's nothing wrong with your eyesight.'

FOOT-IN-MOUTH DISEASE

Often, knowing you're past it coincides with the time you open your mouth and say completely the wrong thing.

One day, an elderly woman was visiting a long-lost relative's house for tea. Her hostess's young son ran up to her as she entered the house and blurted out, 'My, how ugly you are.'

Horrified, the child's mother remonstrated, 'Zack! What do you mean, calling Mrs Winters ugly?'

'I only meant it as a joke,' replied the little boy.

'Well,' said the mother, clearly without thinking through her reply, 'how much better would the joke have been if you had said to our guest, "My, how pretty you are!"'

DON'T ASK MY AGE

One day, the National Census surveyor was doing his rounds. He knocked on Miss Campbell's door. Miss Campbell happily answered all his questions – except one. She wouldn't tell the census man her age.

'Miss Campbell, everyone tells me their age,' he said kindly.

'What? Did Miss Elizabeth Hill and Miss Katie Hill tell you theirs?'

'Yes.'

'Well, I'm the same age as them,' confided Miss Campbell.

So the census taker wrote down: 'As old as the Hills.'

WRONG END OF THE STICK

Lady Constance Milligan was making some final arrangements for a large party she was going to throw that evening.

'Betty,' she said to her loyal housekeeper, 'for the first twenty minutes, I would like it if you'd stand at the drawing-room door and call the guests' names as they arrive.'

Betty's face glowed with pleasure. 'Thank you, madam,' she replied. 'I've been wanting to do that to your friends for the past thirty years.'

TOILET BREAKS

The author John Mortimer certainly knows all about the trials and tribulations of growing old, for as he once said, 'When you get to my age, life seems little more than one long march to and from the lavatory.'

SHHH!

Knowing you're past it is not something you necessarily want the world to know about, or those of a darker persuasion, as this quotation from Nicholas Chamfort, which is reproduced in *The Oxford Book of Ages*, attests.

'A woman of ninety said to M. de Fontenelle, when he was ninety-five: "Death has forgotten us."

' "Shhh!" de Fontenelle answered, putting his finger over his mouth.'

WHAT DID I JUST SAY?

As we all know, life can be a matter of the blind leading the blind, as this letter to *Reader's Digest* clearly demonstrates. Even our teachers are subject to being past it, it seems. Michelle Salter wrote in November 2007:

> During an intensive training course, I said to the instructor, 'I don't know how I'll remember all this information for the test.'
>
> 'I've been using mind-mapping techniques for twenty years to help me memorize things,' he told me. 'Actually, I've run courses on the subject.'
>
> The chat drifted on to other matters, but, intrigued by his mention of his techniques, I approached the instructor over lunch.
>
> 'Do you still do mind-mapping tuition?'
>
> 'Yes, I do,' he said, looking surprised. 'How did you know about that?'

OLD ACTORS

The actor Junius Brutus Booth – father of John Wilkes Booth, who assassinated US president Abraham Lincoln – was to all intents and purposes a rather forgetful fellow.

One day, he was found by the manager of the theatre he was playing at stumbling around the dressing rooms asking, 'Where's the stage and what's the play?'

WRONG DIRECTION

In October 1964, one of the greatest sporting gaffes of all time was perpetrated by American football star Jim Marshall of the Minnesota Vikings.

The Vikings were playing against the San Francisco 49ers, when Marshall suddenly took hold of the ball and began running the *wrong* way up the pitch.

Oblivious to the fact that none of his opponents seemed in any way anxious to stop him and ignoring his own teammates, who were hollering at him to stop or at the very least turn around, Marshall eventually reached the goal line, where he scored two points … for the 49ers.

TIMBER!

In 2001, a tree surgeon suffered a major – and costly – senior moment when it came to embarking on his latest commission.

His client had asked him to cut down a beech tree, the roots of which were damaging the foundations of his property. However, deep in his work, the tree surgeon felled the wrong tree – an irreplaceable ninety-year-old oak!

He was later made to pay his customer a substantial sum in damages after a court decided he was in breach of contract. Being past it was simply no defence.

MISTAKEN IDENTITY

One day, the American writer and comedian Robert Benchley was out to dinner with his son Nathaniel.

'We went to the Trocadero,' writes Nathaniel in his memoir of his father, *Robert Benchley: A Biography*. 'When, in the course of events, we left to go home, he went to a uniformed man at the door and said, "Would you get us a taxi, please?"

'The man turned round and regarded him icily. "I'm very sorry," he said. "I happen to be a rear admiral in the United States Navy."

'"All right, then," said my father. "Get us a battleship."'

YOU KNOW YOU'RE PAST IT WHEN ...

- You receive two invitations to go out on the same night, and choose to attend the event that gets you home the earliest.

- You sit in a rocking chair and can't get it started.

- You muddle up having a clear conscience with having a bad memory.

- You wonder how you could be over the hill when you don't ever remember reaching the top of it.

- You are cautioned to slow down by the doctor instead of the police.

- Travelling isn't as much fun because all the ancient sites are younger than you are.

- Every time you suck in your gut, your ankles swell.

- Your investment in health insurance is finally beginning to pay off.

- Your secrets are safe with your friends – because they can't remember them either.

OVER AND DONE WITH?

Even great men can feel past it. Take the following quote by Disraeli, which appears in *The Oxford Book of Ages*.

'Power? It has come to me too late. There were days when, on waking, I felt I could move dynasties [...]; but that has passed away.'

THREE LETTERS OF LOVE

Three sons grew up, left home, went out on their own and prospered. Meeting up for dinner one night, they discussed the presents they'd given their dear mother for her recent birthday.

The first son said, 'I constructed a mansion for our mother.'

The second said, 'I sent her a BMW with a chauffeur.'

The third smiled and said, 'I've got you both beat. You know how Mum enjoys the Bible? Well, we all know that she can't see too well any more to read it herself. So I bought her a parrot that can recite the entire Bible. It took sixteen nuns in a remote convent eleven years to teach him. I had to pledge to contribute £200,000 a year for a whole decade, but it was worth it. Mum just has to name the chapter and verse, and the parrot will recite it.'

Soon after, the mother penned her letters of thanks and posted them to her children.

'Roger,' she wrote to the first son, 'the mansion you built is so huge. I live in only two rooms, but I have to maintain the entire building.'

'Rory,' she wrote to the second son, 'I am too frail to travel. I stay home all the time, so I never use the BMW. And the chauffeur is so rude!'

'Dearest Randall,' she wrote to her third son, 'you were the only son to have the good sense to know what your mother likes. That chicken was delicious.'

THE DREADED MENOPAUSE

Women sometimes get to know they're past it when their bodies begin giving out increasingly desperate signals – otherwise known as the menopause. Here are a few ways to discover if you are experiencing 'oestrogen issues':

1. Everyone around you has an attitude problem.

2. You're adding chocolate flakes to your savoury pie.

3. The dryer has shrunk every last pair of your trousers.

4. Your husband is suddenly agreeing to everything you say.

5. You're using your mobile phone to dial up every bumper sticker that says: 'How's my driving? Call 0207 …'

HEAVEN-SENT

Bob and Joe are two retired widowers, who reside close to each other and do occasional welfare checks on each other, when they remember.

One day, as he drinks his morning tea, Joe opens the local paper and turns to the Obituaries page. He gets the shock of his life when he sees his own obituary in the column.

He correctly surmises that it's simply a mistaken entry from the paper's database, premature and erroneous. The gaffe still rankles him, so he calls up Bob.

'Bob, are you up yet?'

Bob answers sleepily, 'Yeah, but I'm only now eating my breakfast.'

'Bob, open the newspaper to page 42.'

'Why, what's in the paper?'

'Bob, get the paper and open it to page 42 now!'

'OK, OK, I've got the paper here. So what's on page 42?'

'Bob, open the damn paper to page 42.'

'All right, don't be such a damn pain in the ass so early in the morning. What's on page 42 that's so important?'

'Bob, look at the bottom of column four.'

'Why? What's that story on?'

'Bob, read the damn story on the bottom of the damn column.'

'OK, OK, I'll start reading the damn column if you stop yelling in my ear!'

The paper rustles for a few seconds, then a long pause ensues.

Finally, Bob comes on the line quietly and fearfully. 'So, Joe, where are you calling me from right now?'

MUDDLED UP?

After giving his Sunday sermon, a bishop was standing by the cathedral doors, thanking his congregation as they made their way out, when an enthused lady walked up to him.

'Bishop,' she gushed, 'you'll never know what your service meant to me. It was just like water to a drowning man!'

DO COME IN

During World War I, Prince Louis Esterhazy was in his castle when the large ammunition factory next door exploded. The detonations could be heard for miles around, added to which all the windows in the castle shattered.

Prince Esterhazy, who was sitting in an armchair at the time, shouted, 'Come in!' Apparently, he thought someone was knocking at his door and was delighted that his hearing was good enough to register it!

Doctor:	You're going to live to be sixty.
Patient:	I am sixty!
Doctor:	What did I tell you?

HAIR TODAY ...

If the menopause is a sign that women are past it, surely it follows that baldness is a sign that men aren't quite the youthful creatures they used to be.

Being 'follically challenged' is something that the eminent British philosopher Thomas Hobbes knew all about. In his eighties, Hobbes was almost completely bald, but he wouldn't wear a hat, claiming he never suffered from head colds.

Instead, the biggest problem 'was to keep flies from pitching on the baldness'.

... GONE TOMORROW

Or how about this observation from British comic Dave Barry on how those men who try to cover up their baldness only show themselves to be more past it than most?

'The method preferred by most balding men for making themselves look silly is called the "comb-over", which is when the man grows the hair on one side of his head very long and combs it across the bald area, creating an effect that looks from the top like an egg in the grasp of a large tropical spider.'

'I really don't deserve this,' Jack Benny once remarked, while accepting an award. 'But I have arthritis and I don't deserve that either.'

PRIORITIES

A woman paused in the middle of the street on a very blustery day, using both hands to hold on to her hat as a strong gust of wind blew her dress up around her waist.

A dignified gentleman came up to her and said, 'Ma'am, you should be ashamed of yourself, letting your skirt blow around your middle, being indecent, while both hands hold your hat.'

She said, 'Look, mister, everything down there is as old as I am. This hat is brand new!'

SPLASHING AROUND

According to his wife, novelist G. K. Chesterton was renowned for having odd lapses of memory – none more so than on one particular day when he had gone to take a bath. Standing outside the bathroom door, she heard him get out of the tub, after which there was a long interval and then a loud splashing noise.

Apparently, Chesterton had forgotten that he'd already bathed and had sat back in the bath again.

On realizing his error, his wife then heard him exclaim: 'Damn, I've been here before!'

FUNEREAL MOMENTS

There can be no greater reminder that one is getting on in life than when one's thoughts begin turning to funeral arrangements.

A little before his death, the elderly and somewhat infirm Lord Chesterfield was accustomed to being taken out in his coach and horses. In fact, so infirm was he that the horses were usually made to go at no more than a stepping pace.

One day, while engaged in this activity, a friend came up to Lord Chesterfield's carriage to congratulate the old man on still being able to get out and take the air.

'I thank you kindly, sir,' said his lordship, 'but I do not come out so much for the air, as for the benefit of rehearsing my funeral.'

HOW TO MAKE YOUR CHILDREN
FEEL GUILTY

One weekend, a woman decided to call her father in California because it had been quite some time since they had chatted.

The woman asked her father, 'How are you doing?'

'Not too good,' he said. 'I've been very weak.'

'Pop, why are you so weak?' the daughter asked.

He said, 'Because I haven't eaten anything in thirty-eight days.'

The daughter then asked, 'How come you haven't eaten in thirty-eight days?'

'Because I didn't want my mouth to be filled with food when you called,' he replied.

I *DON'T* NEED YOUR HELP

You definitely know you're past it when complete strangers start helping you to cross the road – even when you don't want them to, which is what happened to the TV character Victor Meldrew in the sitcom *One Foot in the Grave*.

Said Meldrew: 'A young boy down the road tried to help me across the road this afternoon. I gave him a swift cuff round the ear. Only be a matter of time before they're forcing me on a day trip to Eastbourne.'

FOILED BY A STUB

Bank robbers really don't have a lot to remember when they go out on a job, so Kevin Thompson must have thought he was completely past it when, in 1987, he went to rob the Mid-Atlantic National Bank in Bloomfield, New Jersey, but forgot to take his hold-up note with him.

Consequently, he decided to improvise and scrawled his note on the back of one of his cheque stubs, which he then handed to a teller.

After the robbery had taken place, the teller duly handed in the stub to the police. With all the relevant information it provided for them, the cops promptly went straight to Mr Thompson's address and arrested him.

ON GOING GREY

As soon as your hair starts going grey, it's an undeniable sign that your best years are behind you. Scottish comedian Billy Connolly takes this fact to an extreme with his observation on the grey problem.

'I'm so grey,' he says, 'I look like I'm going to rain sometimes. And my pubic hair is going grey. In a certain light, you'd swear it was Stewart Granger down there.'

GRANNY DUTY

While appearing on Channel 4's *The Paul O'Grady Show*, the British comedienne Jo Brand recalled an incident that had befallen her a few days previously, when she had gone to pick up her children from school.

At the school gates, she bumped into an MP, also there to pick up her kids, who asked Brand if she was 'on granny duty today'.

'The cheek!' said Brand. 'I shouldn't name her. But it was Tessa Jowell.'

YOU KNOW YOU'RE PAST IT WHEN ...

- You go to the dictionary to look up a word, spend minutes locating it, then realize you're staring down at the word 'dictionary'.

- You still chase women, but only downhill. – Bob Hope

- Your supply of brain cells is finally down to a size you can handle.

- You fib about your grandchildren's ages.

- Everything hurts and what doesn't hurt, doesn't work.

- The only thing you still retain is water. – Alex Cole

- Your mind makes contracts your body can't keep.

NO FOOL LIKE AN OLD FOOL

A miserly old lawyer who had been diagnosed with a terminal illness was determined to prove wrong the old saying, 'You can't take it with you.'

After much thought and consideration, the old litigator finally devised a way of taking at least some of his money with him when he died. He told his wife to go to the bank and withdraw enough cash to fill two sacks. He then directed her to take the money to the attic and leave it directly above his bed.

His plan: when he passed away, he would reach out and grab the sacks on his way to heaven.

Several weeks after the funeral, the deceased lawyer's wife, up in the attic sorting out his things, came upon the two forgotten sacks stuffed with cash.

'Oh, that old idiot,' she exclaimed. 'I knew he should have had me put the money in the basement.'

TYPOS

Reader's Digest received this letter in December 2007 from a gentleman, Lawrence Dunham, who really hoped he *wasn't* past it.

'To celebrate my retirement, my wife and I dined with a friend we hadn't seen for years. The next day, he sent us an email that included, I hope, a typo: "How wonderful it was to see you both ageing."'

THE SILVER LINING

One benefit of being past it must be that one often lives in one's own befuddled bubble, oblivious to the potentially upsetting things that others might be trying to tell us.

For instance, when Sir Geoffrey Howe was sacked from his position of foreign secretary by the then prime minister, Margaret Thatcher, she told him: 'I'm very sorry, Geoffrey, but I've decided to put John Major in the foreign office.'

To which Howe is supposed to have replied, 'Oh, that's all right. I'm sure he'll be a great help to me.'

HATS OFF

A lady in her forties walked into a milliner's to try on a hat. The sales assistant fawned over her, declaring, 'You look wonderful in that hat. Really, it makes you look ten years younger when you wear it.'

'Then I don't want it,' exclaimed the customer. 'I can't afford to put on ten years every time I take my hat off!'

CROSS YOUR LEGS

A middle-aged lady goes to the bar on a cruise ship and orders a whisky with two drops of water. As the bartender gives her the drink, she says, 'I'm on this cruise to celebrate my birthday and it's today.'

The bartender says, 'Well, since it's your birthday, I'll buy you a drink. In fact, this one is on me.'

As the lady finishes her drink, the man to her left says, 'I would like to buy you a drink, too.'

The birthday gal replies, 'Thank you. Bartender, I want a whisky with two drops of water.'

'Coming right up,' says the bartender.

As she finishes that drink, the young woman to her right says, 'I would like to buy you one, too.'

The lady responds, 'Thank you. Bartender, I want another whisky with two drops of water.'

'Coming right up,' the bartender says. As he gives her the beverage, he asks, 'Ma'am, I'm dying to know. Why the whisky with only two drops of water?'

The lady replies, 'Young man, when you're my age, you've learned how to hold your alcohol. Holding your water, however, is a whole other problem.'

CHANGING TIMES

The actor John Barrymore was once asked by a young newspaper reporter whether acting still gave him as much pleasure as it had in his early career.

'Young man, I am seventy-five,' Barrymore replied. 'Nothing is as much fun as it used to be!'

CURIOUSER AND CURIOUSER

The British author and humorist Alan Coren was a great one for witty observations, particularly on growing older.

'There are many mysteries in old age,' he once wrote, 'but the greatest, surely, is this: in those adverts for walk-in bathtubs, why doesn't all the water gush out when you get in?'

FORGOTTEN STORIES

Sebastian and Fred, who were both in their early fifties, were sitting on a park bench, enjoying the sunshine and catching up with one another.

'So, Seb, what's new with you?' asked Fred.

Seb looked a little bit troubled. 'To be honest,' he replied, 'I had a really great story I wanted to tell you, but I've already forgotten it.'

'Oh,' said Fred, 'well, if it's about "forgotten stories", I have a better one to tell you than that … if only I could remember it!'

PINK NIPPLES?

Tory leader David Cameron must really have felt he was past it when interviewer Jeremy Paxman bamboozled him with the following questions: 'Do you know what a Pink Pussy is? Do you know what a Slippery Nipple is?'

The answer was regrettably 'no', on both counts.

IN VERY BAD TASTE

A funeral service is being held for a woman who has just died. At the end of the ceremony, the pall-bearers are carrying the casket out of the church when they bump into a wall. They hear a quiet moan! They open the casket and find that the woman is actually still alive. She lives for six more years, and then dies.

Once again, a service is held, and at the end of it, the pall-bearers are again carrying out the casket. As they near the door, the husband cries out: 'Watch that wall!'

YOU KNOW YOU'RE PAST IT WHEN ...

- You buy a sheer, sexy negligée, but you don't know anyone whose eyesight is good enough to see through it.

- Job interviewers no longer ask you, 'What do you think you'll be doing in ten years' time?'

- You have your own phone number written down somewhere, but can't remember where.

- Your favourite section of the paper is 'On This Date Fifty Years Ago'.

- Conversations with people your own age often turn into 'duelling ailments'.

- You're on a TV game show and decide to risk it all and go for the chairlift.

- You're seventeen around the neck, forty-one around the waist, and ninety-five around the golf course.

- You have too much room in the house and not enough room in the medicine cabinet.

SILLY OLD JOKE
Old owls never die, they just don't give a hoot!

SUICIDAL THOUGHTS

A mature widow is distraught after the death of her faithful spouse. She can't live without him and decides that the best way to do herself in is to stab herself in her pitifully broken heart. Still, she doesn't want to mess it up, so she calls a doctor to find out exactly where the heart is.

He tells her to put her first two fingers together, hold them horizontally and place the tip of the first finger just below her left nipple. The heart, he says, is immediately below the first knuckle on her second finger.

Later that day, the doctor is called to Casualty to put thirteen stitches in the woman's left thigh.

LITTLE WHITE LIES ...

One day, Archie rushes in to see his GP.

'Doctor, you *have* to prescribe me something to make me feel young again. I've got a date with a gorgeous woman this evening and I'm in urgent need of a pep-me-up.'

His doctor looks at Archie for a long time, and then says honestly, 'Archie, you're in your eighties – there's not a great deal I can do for you.'

'But, Doctor,' replies Archie, 'my friend Reg is much older than I am and he says he makes love to his girlfriend five or six times a week.'

'OK,' says the doctor, 'so you say it too!'

YOU KNOW YOU'RE PAST IT
WHEN … YOU DIE ON THE JOB

John Entwistle, bass guitarist with The Who, died in 2002 while in bed with a stripper. Lead singer of the group, Roger Daltrey, commented that he'd miss his friend and fellow band member, but added:

'Ask any man what he would prefer: to live to a ripe old age and die alone, or to go out shagging your balls off with strippers in Vegas. Come on, let's be honest. It's not a death that any man should be ashamed of.'

BY MY CALCULATIONS

Three befuddled men are at their local surgery for a test. The doctor asks the first man, 'What is three times three?'

'560,' is his reply.

The doctor is exasperated, but he has hope for the other patients. He says to the second man, 'It's your turn. What is three times three?'

'Saturday,' replies the second man.

The doctor tuts, and tells the third man, 'OK, your turn. What's three times three?'

'Nine,' responds the third man.

'Fantastic!' exclaims the doctor. 'Well done! How did you get that?'

'Simple,' he replies, 'just subtract 560 from Saturday.'

SOME VERY WISE WORDS

Curly-haired, angelic-looking Harpo Marx, whose other trademarks included playing the harp and never speaking on film, was one of the famous Marx brothers (alongside Chico and Groucho). Loved by millions all over the world for the films he and his brothers made, off screen he was no less humorous – particularly when it came to making fun of old age.

'Many years ago,' he wrote in his autobiography, 'a very wise man named Bernard Baruch took me aside and put his arm around my shoulder.

'"Harpo, my boy," he said, "I'm going to give you three pieces of advice, three things you should always remember."

'My heart jumped and I glowed with expectation. I was going to hear the magic password to a rich, full life from the master himself.

'"Yes, sir?" I said. And he told me the three things.

'I regret I've forgotten what they were.'

OH CAROL!

According to an anecdote told by Truman Capote in *Answered Prayers* (1986), the Hollywood actor Walter Matthau was once at a party with his wife Carol, when she overheard him talking to an elderly woman who, as Carol described her, was 'mutton dressed as lamb'.

Apparently, Walter was then overheard asking, 'How old are you?' At which point, Carol butted in and said, 'Why don't you saw off her legs and count the rings?'

OLD GERTRUDE

This next anecdote was first told by Robin Bailey on BBC Radio 4's wonderful programme *Quote ...Unquote* on 27 July 1985.

Robert Helpman was said one day to have gone to see a touring production of *Hamlet*, when he noticed that the actress playing Gertrude was perhaps a little older than she really should have been for the role.

'I hope they cut that line about "Go not to thy uncle's bed",' he was overheard to say, 'because, frankly, she'd never make it.'

SPEAK YOUR MIND

A forthright connoisseur of culture, whose increasing years had made her increasingly frank, was among a group looking at an art exhibition in a newly opened gallery. Suddenly, one contemporary painting caught her eye.

'What on earth,' she enquired of the artist standing nearby, 'is that?'

He smiled condescendingly. 'That, my dear lady, is supposed to be a cow and its calf.'

'Well, then,' snapped the woman in reply, 'why isn't it?'

NOTHING LIKE A GOOD MEMORY

Being old is sometimes a fantastic disguise. People assume that you're frail and decrepit, that your mind is full of holes and your bladder full of urine. But, on occasion, a razor-sharp wit nestles beneath the chapped tongue, and a fine brain resides in the grey-haired head.

A small-town prosecuting attorney called his first witness to the stand in a trial – a grandmotherly woman who had long been a respected member of the local community. He approached her and asked, 'Mrs Pickford, do you know me?'

She responded, 'Why, yes, I do know you, Mr Moore. I've known you since you were a child. And frankly, you've been a big disappointment to me. You lie, you cheat on your girlfriend, you manipulate people and talk about them behind their backs. You think you're a big shot when you haven't the brains to realize you will never amount to anything more than a two-bit paper pusher. Yes, I know you.'

The lawyer was stunned. Not knowing what else to do, he pointed across the room and asked, 'Mrs Pickford, do you know the defence attorney?'

She again replied, 'Why, yes, I do. I've known Mr Pearce since he was a youngster, too. I used to babysit him for his parents. And he, too, has been a real disappointment to me. He's lazy, prejudiced, he has a gambling problem. The man can't build a good relationship with anyone and his estate is one of the shoddiest in the entire neighbourhood. Yes, I know him.'

At this point, the judge rapped the courtroom to

silence and called both counsellors to the bench. In a very quiet voice, he said with menace, 'If either of you asks her if she knows me, you'll be in jail for contempt before you can draw breath!'

FLASH HARRY

Even flashers must experience days when they feel over the hill – take the following story, for example.

A lone woman is walking through the Garment District in New York when suddenly a man walks up to her, blocks her path and opens up his raincoat, under which he is completely naked.

Unperturbed by the sight, the fashion aficionado looks him up and down, and then remarks, 'This you call a lining?'

FINISHED YET?

Going on and on and on is often a good indication that you are past it. After all, part of the art of giving a good speech is knowing exactly when to stop – hence the inclusion of the following joke.

'Has he finished yet?' asked a victim of a particularly long oration being given by an elderly professor at Oxford.

'Yes,' came his companion's reply. 'He finished a long time ago, but he just won't stop.'

ROUGH DAY

'It's been a rough day. I got up this morning, put on a shirt and a button fell off. I picked up my briefcase and the handle came off. I'm afraid to go to the bathroom.'

RODNEY DANGERFIELD

ANOTHER CASE OF FOOT-IN-MOUTH DISEASE

One day, Mrs Cholmondely was entertaining at home and employed a famous violinist to entertain her guests. When the musician had finished his recital, everyone crowded around him.

'I must be honest,' said one of the guests, 'I'm afraid I thought your performance was awful.'

Quickly, Mrs Cholmondely interrupted: 'Oh don't pay any attention to him. He hasn't the slightest idea what he's talking about. He only repeats what he hears everyone else saying!'

OLD FROGS

One of the saddest things about feeling past it is that it can be one of the loneliest times in life. A middle-aged lady decided that she needed a pet to keep her company, so off to the pet shop she went – but nothing seemed to catch her interest, except a rather ugly frog.

As she walked by the cage he was sitting in, he seemed to look up and wink at her. She could have sworn he whispered, 'I'm lonely too, buy me and you won't be sorry,' but she knew her hearing was no longer good enough for whispers, so she didn't pay any attention.

As nothing else was even of vague interest, she bought the frog and walked dejectedly to her car.

As they were driving down the road, however, she heard the frog whisper again. 'Kiss me, you won't be sorry,' he croaked.

With nothing to lose, the woman thought, 'What the heck,' and gave the frog a peck on his scaly lips.

Immediately, the reptile turned into an absolutely stunning, delectable young prince. Then the prince kissed her back, and you know what the woman turned into?

The first motel she could find.

GETTING THE SNIP

One of the clearest signs of ageing for men is when their libido drops or, worse still, when they become impotent.

Such was obviously the case for Irish poet W. B. Yeats, who at the age of sixty-nine not only suffered from this condition in the bedroom, but also thought it prevented him from producing new work.

Fed up with this state of affairs, he decided to undergo an operation developed by Austrian doctor Eugen Steinach (1861–1944), which was in effect a vasectomy, because in those days people believed that a vasectomy would increase one's testosterone levels and subsequently one's virility.

Naturally, the operation didn't work – but Yeats did feel rejuvenated enough to pick up his pen again, so at least some good came of it!

YOU KNOW YOU'RE PAST IT WHEN …

- You've got more bottles in your medicine cabinet than you have in your wine cellar.

- You run out of breath walking *down* a flight of stairs.

- You choose your films by how comfy the seats are in each cinema.

- Even your birthday suit needs pressing. – Bob Hope

- You can still fill your own car up with oil, but you can't remember how to open the bonnet.

- You look both ways before crossing a room.

- You stoop to tie your shoelaces and wonder what else you could do while you're down there. – Geroge Burns

- Your idea of exercise is bending over to pick up your wig.

- You arrive home from the airport by taxi to discover your car has been stolen, only for the police to phone up and tell you they've found it right where you parked it back at the airport.

> 'You know you're getting old when you start to like your mum and dad again. Yes, Mum, I'd love to come caravanning to Tenby with you. No, I'll bring a packed lunch. I'm not paying café prices.'
>
> JEFF GREEN

SNOOZING

It's hard to know sometimes exactly who is the one who's past it, but I think in this next anecdote the clergyman is the one left with most egg on his face ...

After a very long and rather tedious Sunday service at her local church, a middle-aged woman approached the minister and shook his hand.

'Reverend,' she exclaimed, 'I do apologize for dozing off during your sermon.

'But,' she added succinctly, 'I want you to know I didn't miss a thing.'

HELICOPTER RIDE

Charlie and his wife Deborah went to the state fair every year. They'd wander the stalls and take in the sights, and every year Charlie would say hopefully, 'Deborah, I'd like to ride in that helicopter.'

But Debbie always talked him down. 'I know, Charlie,' she'd say, 'but that helicopter ride is fifty dollars – and fifty dollars is fifty dollars.'

One year, as usual, they went to the fair, but Charlie was determined that this trip would be different. He said firmly to his wife, 'Deborah, I'm sixty-five years old. If I don't ride that helicopter now, I might never get another chance.'

Deborah pointed out, 'Charlie, that helicopter ride is fifty dollars – and fifty dollars is fifty dollars.'

The pilot happened to overhear the couple's quarrel and stepped in to play the peacemaker – but with a mischievous glint in his eye. He said, 'Folks, I'll make you a deal. I'll take the both of you for a ride. If you can stay quiet for the entire ride and not say a word, I won't charge you. But if you say one word, it's fifty dollars.'

Charlie and Deborah agreed and the flight began. The pilot took the opportunity to perform all kinds of fancy manoeuvres, but he didn't hear a peep from his passengers, not even when they loop the looped. He executed his daredevil tricks over and over again, but still not a word.

When they landed, the pilot turned round to Charlie and exclaimed, 'That's amazing. I did everything I possibly could to make you yell out, but you didn't – not once. I'm impressed!

Charlie responded, 'Well, to be quite honest, I almost said something when Debbie fell out, but you know – fifty dollars is fifty dollars.'

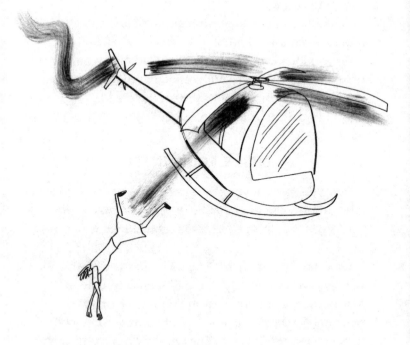

GLAD TIDINGS

A sixty-year-old woman was walking along when she heard a voice from above: 'You will live to be a hundred.' She looked around and didn't see anyone. Again, she heard: 'You will live to be a hundred.'

'Oh,' she thought to herself, 'that was the voice of God. I've got forty more years to live!'

So off she went to the plastic surgeon. She got her whole body fixed up – face lift, boob job, bottom lift, liposuction, Botox, collagen, nose. You name it, it was now transformed.

As soon as she left the surgeon's office, she got hit by a car, passed away and finally ascended to heaven.

She said to God accusingly, 'You told me I would live to be a hundred. I was supposed to have had forty more years. So how come you let the car kill me?'

God said, 'I didn't recognize you.'

LITTLE ACCIDENTS

When you start having little accidents of the urinary kind, it's a sure signal that the years are really creeping up on you. But this next story takes that to a whole new level.

One day, the English actress Mrs Patrick Campbell, who was carrying her pet dog Moonbeam in her arms, hailed down a London taxicab. At first, the driver didn't want to take the pair in his car, but Campbell climbed in nonetheless and ordered, 'The Empire Theatre, my man, and no nonsense!'

On the way there, however, Moonbeam disgraced himself on the floor of the cab, leading the driver to point out the large puddle now soiling his vehicle.

But Mrs Campbell wouldn't hear a word of it. 'Moonbeam didn't pee,' she said, '*I* did.'

SPEAK ENGLISH?

John and Mary-Beth rarely left their native Florida, but when their son married a Portuguese girl, they jumped at the chance to visit Europe.

'But we don't speak Portuguese,' fretted Mary-Beth.

'No problem,' John replied, 'they'll speak English like the rest of the world.'

They arrived in Portugal at the height of summer and the first thing John wanted was a cold beer. They found a restaurant and beckoned a waiter.

'I'd like a beer, please,' said John. The waiter looked puzzled, but John pressed on. 'And I'd like it cold.'

The waiter's brow became more furrowed. Sensing he was not getting his message across, John did what he thought was the norm for visitors to foreign countries – he added an 'o' to the English. 'Coldo,' he explained loudly.

At this, the waiter's face brightened. '*Sim, senhor*,' he said and hurried off to the kitchen.

Five minutes later, he returned – not with a refreshing cold beer, but with hot chilli soup. John had learned his first word of Portuguese: '*caldo*' means 'broth'.

HERE WE GO AGAIN

A group of Canadians were travelling by tour bus through Holland. They stopped at a cheese farm, where a young guide led them through the process of cheese making, explaining that goat's milk was used.

She showed the group a hillside, on which many goats were grazing. 'These,' she explained 'are the older goats put out to pasture when they no longer produce.'

She then asked, 'What do you do in Canada with your old goats?'

A sprightly old gentleman answered, 'They send us on coach tours!'

DO YOU KNOW WHO YOU ARE?

Amongst all the excellent collection of quotes, quips and anecdotes that Jacob Braude included in his *Toastmaster's Handbook*, the following story is the perfect example of someone receiving due warning that he was definitely on his way to getting old.

'The man in the barber's chair was comfortably emulsified under a pack of steaming towels, when suddenly a boy rushed into the shop, shouting, "Mr Balsam, Mr Balsam, your store is on fire!"

'Horrified, the customer leaped from his chair, ripped off the apron and sped wildly up the street. After two or three blocks, he stopped suddenly, scratched his head and cried out in great perplexity: "What in the heck am I doing? My name isn't Balsam."'

CHOP, CHOP

The stereotypical middle-aged spinster with a fondness for felines was sitting in front of the fire with her favourite tomcat on her knee. Suddenly, there was a loud bang, a puff of smoke, and a twinkling fairy appeared out of the fire.

'I can grant you three wishes,' the fairy announced. 'What would you like?'

When she had recovered from the shock, the pragmatic woman answered, 'Given the credit crunch, I would firstly like to be financially secure and live in comfortable surroundings till the end of my days.'

With a flick of her wand, the fairy turned the room

into a splendid parlour and produced an array of sacks of gold.

'Next wish, please,' she said.

'Please make me young and beautiful,' pleaded the downtrodden senior, and she was immediately transformed into a beautiful brunette. 'For my third wish, will you please turn my tomcat into a handsome young man?'

Instantly, standing before her was a fine specimen of manhood, who stepped forward and took the lady's hand and kissed it, saying, 'Aren't you sorry now that you took me to the vet?'

ALWAYS LOOK ON THE BRIGHT SIDE

The best thing about being senile is that you can hide your own Easter eggs and be surprised by the Christmas presents you've bought yourself.

SEVENTY-FIVE AGAIN!

One day in 1994, the actor and comedian Victor Borge announced, 'I'm celebrating my seventy-fifth birthday, which is sort of embarrassing, because I'm eighty-five.'

A QUESTION OF PATERNITY

A couple are having an intimate meal to celebrate their fiftieth wedding anniversary.

The man leans forward and softly says to his wife, 'Dear, there is something that I must ask you. It has always troubled me that our ninth child never looked quite like the rest of our brood. Now, I want to assure you that these fifty years have been the most wonderful experience, and your answer cannot take that away. But I must know, did he have a different father?'

The wife drops her head in shame, unable to look her husband straight in the eye. She pauses for a moment, then she replies, 'Yes. Yes he did.'

The man is shaken. The truth of what his wife is admitting hits him very hard.

With a lump in his throat, he asks, 'Who? Who was he? Who was the father?'

Again, the woman hangs her head, saying nothing at first, as she tries to muster the courage to tell her husband the truth.

Then, finally, she says, 'You.'

HEAD IN THE CLOUDS

Plenty of us know we're past it when our looks begin to fade and our bodies begin to crumble or wizen or both, but for some people, it's when the simple things in life start to become really puzzling.

Hastings Randall, who was a moral philosopher and theologian at New College, Oxford in the early twentieth century, was one day found by an undergraduate pumping up the front wheel of his bicycle. Said the student to Randall, 'Excuse me, sir, but that will do no good.'

Hastings Randall asked why.

'Because it's your back tyre that is flat,' replied the student.

'Goodness me,' said Randall, 'do you mean to tell me they're not connected?'

TO EAT OR NOT TO EAT

The Nobel Prize-winning chemist Harold Urey (1893–1981), who was famed for his forgetfulness, was stopped in the street by a friend of his one sunny afternoon. After a brief conversation, the men began to go their separate ways – until, that is, Urey turned round and asked: 'John, which way was I walking when I met you?'

His friend pointed in the right direction.

'Oh good,' said Urey, 'that means I've already had my lunch!'

LADIES AND GENTLEMEN

Not knowing where you are is usually the preserve of explorers who have lost their compass and maps, but occasionally, it is an early indication that you are past it, as the following anecdote testifies.

A woman entered a room in a London hotel, where she immediately recognized a well-known British politician pacing up and down, up and down. The woman asked the gentleman what he was doing there.

'I'm about to give an after-dinner speech,' he said.

'And do you always get so nervous before you are called upon to deliver them?' she asked, not unreasonably.

'Nervous?' he replied. 'I'm not nervous. In fact, I never get nervous.'

'Then what are you doing,' demanded the woman, 'in the ladies' room?'

NOT FEELING YOURSELF?

Often, it's your attitude to life that reveals you as being old and grey, and there comes a time when moaning about the world around us suddenly becomes a daily occurrence.

This is obviously the case for ex-member of the rock group Yes, Rick Wakeman. At one time in his life, Wakeman was very cutting-edge, but now he reveals, 'My band call me Victor Meldrew. My kids call me Victor Meldrew. I actually think that when my hair finally falls out, I'll find that I probably am Victor Meldrew.'

CLUELESS

The American actor John Barrymore was very fond of recalling the confusion that often overran the old stock company with which he had once toured the country playing repertory. Every week, the actors would have to perform a vast array of plays – sometimes doing three different scripts per day.

Naturally, this led to a great deal of befuddlement, but one evening, the absurdity of the situation grew to preposterous proportions. Barrymore, feeling a little past it, found he couldn't remember his lines so, sidling over to the wings, he hissed to the director, 'What's the line? What's the line?'

Wearily, the director looked up, shrugged his shoulders and asked, 'What's the play?'

FEISTY

Feisty to the end, transcendental philosopher Henry David Thoreau was absolute proof that the older you grow, the more belligerent you become.

Towards his twilight years, he was asked if he'd like to make his peace with God.

'I did not know that we had ever quarrelled,' he replied frostily.

TOOTHLESS

Losing one's teeth is no laughing matter. Regrettably, the older one gets, the more likely it is to occur.

The writer James Stern recalled that he and W. H. Auden used to 'have a race as to which of us would be the first to lose all his teeth. I forget who won, but it was a near thing. He had just acquired his first set [of dentures] when – at a Boston tea party given in his honour by a group of elderly ladies – the hostess asked him to extinguish the flame under the silver kettle. Wystan, now forty-five and far from thinking, filled his lungs to capacity. And blew!

'"My dear, the *din*!" exclaimed Auden later. "My uppers went crashing into my neighbour's empty teacup!"'

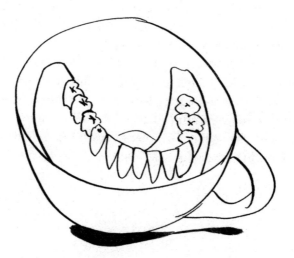

TELL ME WHY I DON'T LIKE COFFEE SHOPS

Sir Bob Geldof, once such a rebellious fellow, now spends his time complaining about the decor in Starbucks, among other things. He has clearly fallen victim to the malaise that strikes us all in our later years: the need to moan about every single aspect of life itself.

'Starbucks makes pretty good coffee. That's got to be a good thing. But it's all those newspapers and "Hey wow" coffee sofas, and the *pain au raisin* that goes with it that I can't stand,' rages Sir Bob. 'So the fact that you can get a decent cup of coffee in any high street – a good thing. All the bollocks that goes with it – f**k off.'

ECONOMICS

Rachel had just become a widow and needed to put an obituary in the local rag about her late husband, Sam. She called the newspaper and asked, 'How much does it cost to put an obituary in the paper?'

'The cost is 60 cents per word,' replied the editor.

Rachel said, 'Fine. Please print: "Sam died."'

The astonished editor explained that there was an eight-word minimum charge. Rachel thought for a moment, then said, 'OK, please print: "Sam died. 1983 pick-up truck now for sale."'

DEAR OLD MICHAEL

While recalling her early courtship with actor Michael Douglas, who is twenty-five years older than her, the actress Catherine Zeta-Jones commented to *Esquire* magazine:

> We were at his house in Spain. It's a beautiful place in Majorca, very remote. And yet they [the press] still find access, the paparazzi, even if they have to rappel down the goddamn mountain. They photographed me and Michael kissing. It was all over the news-stands. And, yes, I was topless and on top of him!
>
> When my father and Michael first met, he said to Michael, 'What were you doing with my daughter in Spain and she's topless?' And Michael said to my dad, 'Well, you know, David, I'm just glad she was on top, since gravity works better for her than it does me!'

WE ALL FALL DOWN

Chat-show host Jay Leno clearly has all his mental faculties intact. The quick-witted presenter once remarked: 'The University of Nebraska says that elderly people that drink beer or wine at least four times a week have the highest bone density. They need it – they're the ones falling down most.'

YOU KNOW YOU'RE PAST IT WHEN ...

- You can't take out a thirty-year mortgage.

- You become obsessed with the thermostat. – Jeff Foxworthy

- You go on a summer holiday and pack a sweater. – Denis Norden

- You start calling your offspring by the dog's name.

- You realize that a stamp today costs more than a picture show did when you were growing up.

- You put on two pounds eating an olive.

- Your short-term memory has been replaced by a notepad and pen ... but you can't remember where you put them.

- You know all medical terms and burial sites.

- You have more fingers on your hands than real teeth in your mouth. – Rodney Dangerfield

MARITAL IGNORANCE IS BLISS

An Australian hoping to move to Hawaii with his Hawaiian wife in 2008 forgot that he had married someone else thirty years earlier. US immigration officials ruled his latest marriage invalid, but despite being shown his signature on the 1978 licence, the man had no recollection of the ceremony. He did, however, vaguely remember a 'nice' blonde from Arizona around that time ...

LETTING YOURSELF GO

Women definitely know they are getting past it when they spend more and more hours each week at the beauty salon, trying to stave off old age.

For example, the American novelist and screenwriter Nora Ephron writes: 'I am only about eight hours a week away from looking like a bag lady, with the frizzled, flyaway grey hair I would probably have if I stopped dying mine; with a pot belly I would definitely develop if I ate just half of what I think about eating every day; with the dirty nails and chapped lips and moustache and bushy eyebrows that would be my destiny if I ever spent two weeks on a desert island.'

HIS BARK IS WORSE THAN HIS BITE

Here's another story about a rather forgetful gentleman. According to a news item posted on a German website, a mature shoplifter in Braunschweig, Germany tried to evade being arrested by two security guards by biting them.

However, pensioner Gustav Ernegger had forgotten to put in his dentures – as a result of which, all he was able to leave was a gummy red mark.

Said police spokesman Gunther Brauner: 'He tried to bite the officer several times, but had forgotten to put his false teeth in and so was unable to cause him any harm.'

DRINK UP

Alfred Lord Tennyson, who was Poet Laureate between the years 1850 and 1892, was renowned for his absent-mindedness, particularly as he grew older, and so it was one evening when he was entertaining the actor Henry Irving at dinner.

After the meal, the two men began to share a decanter of port. Although Irving was given one glass of the beverage, the butler then placed the rest of the bottle in front of Tennyson, who proceeded to refill his own glass, but not Irving's, until the whole bottle was finished.

Tennyson then asked the butler to bring a second bottle to the table. Again Irving's glass was filled once, but thereafter Tennyson drank the rest of the bottle himself.

The following morning, Irving found Tennyson standing by his bed. 'Ah,' said the Poet Laureate, 'but pray, Mr Irving, do you always drink two bottles of port after dinner?'

SIGNS YOU'RE GETTING OLD

Spotting that you're getting old can be a fine art. The character Sophia Petrillo came up with a couple of bona fide indicators for impending demise in the American comedy *The Golden Girls*, when she listed these sure-fire signs, 'One: your children start visiting during the week. Two: your doctor won't let you postdate a cheque.'

THE LETTERS PAGE

Another symptom of growing old is our predilection for writing to national newspapers, complaining about something, writing to complain about people who complain, or simply passing on words of wisdom gained from many years of experience.

This letter to *The Oldie* is a veritable gem from a savvy senior.

> What's all the fuss about being asked one's date of birth? The answer is easy – just do as I do and lie. As far as I know, there's no law that says you can't pretend to be a forgetful old bag. Live up to the expectations of John Q. Public about elderly dottiness when it suits you.
>
> MARGARET LOVE (*The Oldie*, April 2008)

CUP OF TEA?

Adam Smith, author of *The Wealth of Nations*, must have felt he was old before his time when he once placed a slice of bread and butter into a teapot instead of tea leaves and, having poured in boiling water and tasted the brew, declared it the worst cup of tea he had ever had the displeasure of drinking.

DON'T MESS WITH ME, SONNY

A property tycoon was backing his Bentley into the last available parking space when a zippy blue convertible whipped in behind him to take the spot. The twenty-something driver leaped out and said, 'Sorry, Pops, but you've got to be young and smart to do that.'

The tycoon paid no attention to the remark and simply kept reversing until his Bentley had crushed the sports car into a crumpled heap.

'Sorry, son, you've got to be old and rich to do that!'

DEADLY HUMOUR

A middle-aged accountant was laid up in hospital for weeks on end. All the doctors on the ward couldn't seem to help her or diagnose what was wrong.

'Never mind,' said the lady, who simply wanted to get back to her books and her numbers, 'I don't need your help.'

But despite her objections, the doctors still kept trying to get to the bottom of what was making her ill. Finally, when all the medics had left the ward, the lady's relatives asked her what had been decided.

'It's just like I told everyone,' she said triumphantly. 'I'm fine. The doctors, they used all sorts of long complicated words, which I didn't understand, but then they finally said, "Well, there's no use worrying about it or arguing over it. The autopsy will soon give us the answer!"'

BENEFITS

A retired gentleman went to apply for Social Security. After waiting in line for what seemed an eternity, he was finally able to present himself at the relevant desk. The woman behind the counter asked him for his passport to verify his age. The man searched his pockets and realized with a sinking heart that he had left his wallet and all his ID at home.

'Will I have to go home and come back now?' he asked, giving a slightly pathetic sigh.

The woman paused and then said, 'Unbutton your shirt.'

The man opened his shirt, revealing lots of grey chest hair.

The woman said, 'That silver hair is proof enough for me,' and she processed his application.

When he got back home, the man told his wife all about his experience at the Social Security office. She responded, 'You should have dropped your pants – you might have qualified for disability, too.'

THE UNDERWEAR DEBATE

If you want to know whether you're past it or not, ask yourself this: does the underwear you buy for yourself disappoint you to the extent that you would write to the manufacturer or to a newspaper to complain about it? If the answer is 'yes', then I'm afraid you're definitely on your way to senility. After all, aren't there more important things to be worrying about?

Not according to broadcaster and journalist Jeremy Paxman, who, in a private email (which was later leaked to the press) to Stuart Rose, head of Marks & Spencer, laid bare some issues he had with M&S underwear:

> Like very large numbers of men in this country, I have always bought my socks and pants in Marks and Sparks. I've noticed that something very troubling has happened. There's no other way to put this. Their pants no longer provide adequate support.
>
> When I've discussed this with friends and acquaintances, it has revealed widespread gusset anxiety.
>
> The other thing is socks. Even among those of us who clip our toenails very rigorously, they appear to be wearing out much more quickly on the big toe.
>
> Also, they are no longer ribbed around the top, which means they do not stay up in the way they used to. These are matters of great concern to the men in Britain.

Nor, it seems, is Mr Paxman alone in his inability to come to terms with modern underwear. Take, for instance, the following rant by Lindsay Keir Wise, which appeared in *The Oldie* magazine in April 2008:

> I am sure that I speak for others in what is a very sensitive matter. The subject of my dissatisfaction is men's underpants [...] When donning pants, one must ascertain (a) which is the inside and which is the outside and (b) which is the front and which is the back. In doing this, one is guided by the label at the back of the garment [...]
>
> In the cause of sartorial advancement, prompted no doubt by the endorsement of a Beckham or Britney, pants manufacturers have taken to applying the label, hitherto the mark of orientation, not to the inside back but to the *outside front*! This intervention has disturbed the even tenor of my ways: I have not only found my underpants are inside out, but – if called to a public facility – that the exit hole is at the back ...

DO YOU REMEMBER ME?

According to *Braude's Handbook*, Winston Churchill had the perfect riposte for those indiscreet enough to ask, 'Do you remember me?'

Sir Winston always replied, 'Why should I?'

KEEP DEATH OFF THE ROADS

After reserving her seventy-five-year-old grandfather a seat on a flight from New York to Florida, Jane called the airline to go over his special needs. The representative listened patiently as Jane requested a wheelchair and an attendant for her granddad because of his arthritis and impaired vision to the point of near blindness.

Jane's apprehension lightened a bit when the assistant promised her that everything would be taken care of, so she sincerely expressed her gratitude for the good service.

'Oh, you're welcome,' the representative replied.

Jane was about to hang up when the woman cheerfully asked, 'And will your grandfather need a rental car?'

PICTURE IMPERFECT

A picture researcher received a particularly difficult request from a client, but was keen to reply in a positive manner and prove that she was willing to go the extra mile.

However, while drafting her response, she accidentally leaned on her keyboard and ended up typing !!$%%&**!££!*%$**&!£%*! She was so flustered at having written what read like an expletive that in her haste to delete the message, she compounded the error by sending it.

NAUGHTY OLD MAN

A long-suffering wife came home one lunchtime and found her husband of many years amorously involved with a young floozy in the bedroom. The woman was understandably outraged, especially as she had not had a whisper of physical affection from her spouse in a very, very long time. She had in all honesty thought him impotent.

During the quarrel that resulted, she pushed her husband off the balcony of their seventeenth-floor apartment. She was charged with murder and tried.

'But Your Honour,' she said, 'I didn't mean to hurt him.'

'You didn't mean to hurt him?' the judge asked. 'Ma'am, you pushed him off the balcony from the seventeenth floor.'

'Yes,' she said, 'but all those things I had just seen him doing, I thought if he could do them, surely he could fly!'

HOW UNCOOL

Hip-hop rapper and actor LL Cool J was once asked in an interview if he still expected to be rapping in thirty years' time.

'We'll see what Vegas is paying,' he said. 'I'll be rapping about denture cream, Preparation H. My pants will still be sagging – but it'll be from Depends [incontinence pads]!'

HARD OF HEARING

A couple are driving cross-country and the woman is at the wheel. She gets pulled over by the highway patrol.

The officer walks over to her car and says, 'Ma'am, did you know you were speeding?'

The woman turns to her husband and asks, 'What did he say?'

The man yells, 'HE SAYS YOU WERE SPEEDING.'

The patrolman says, 'May I see your licence, please?'

The woman turns to her husband and asks, 'What did he say?'

The man yells, 'HE WANTS TO SEE YOUR DRIVER'S LICENCE.'

The woman gives him her licence.

The patrolman says, 'I see you are from Texas. I spent some time there once. Had the worst sex with a woman I have ever had.'

The woman turns to her husband and asks, 'What did he say?'

The man yells, 'HE THINKS HE KNOWS YOU.'

AN HONEST DAY'S WORK

Some people aren't cut out for a life of crime, as is aptly demonstrated by the following news story about a thief who stormed into a Kansas Kwik Shop in Topeka, USA.

On finding that there wasn't enough cash in the till, he tied up the shop assistant … and then worked the till himself for three hours, before police turned up and arrested him.

WHO'S PAST IT?

Chefs are not renowned for their forgetfulness, but one short-order cook was obviously feeling past it on the day a couple of teenagers walked into his restaurant and ordered two hamburgers.

All morning long, the chef, Simon Martin, had been shouting at the restaurant's waitresses because they kept forgetting to take his orders to the tables. He prided himself on serving up meals as speedily as possible, so he was concerned that their sluggishness reflected badly on him.

Yet pride, it seems, comes before a fall. After the two young men had placed their order, Martin quickly executed the dishes and rang the bell to alert the waiting staff that the food was ready. Imagine how happy the waitresses were when, having promptly served up the meals to the two boys, the pair complained that the chef had forgotten to put the burgers inside the buns!

YOU KNOW YOU'RE PAST IT WHEN ...

- The creaking in your house is coming from your knees.

- There's nothing left to learn the hard way.

- Your TV is as loud as it can get and you still can't hear it.

- You no longer reach for the moon. In fact, you have difficulty reaching for your toes.

- You find yourself beginning to like accordion music.

- You realize time's a great healer, but it's a lousy beautician.

- Your little black book only contains names ending in M.D.

- Your broad mind and your narrow waist begin to change places. – E. Cossman

NAUGHTY OLD GROUCHO!

At seventy years old, Groucho Marx once commented on the Indian summer he was enjoying as an actor.

'I'm going to Iowa for an award,' he said. 'Then I'm appearing at Carnegie Hall. It's sold out. Then I'm sailing to France to be honoured by the French government.'

He paused and added: 'I'd give it all up for one erection.'

UNDERLAY

In 2008, in a hopeful attempt to save money, Nicola Williams of Port Isaac, Cornwall, decided to lay a new carpet in her bedroom with her own fair hands.

She pulled up the old carpet before smoothly laying down the replacement – but, unable to locate her glasses at the crucial moment, didn't notice that she'd buried her dog's favourite squeaky leek beneath the new shag pile. (The strange bulge under the floor went quite unnoticed to her myopic eyes.)

Two days and much barking later, the toy was finally retrieved.

THE MARCH OF TIME

Long-windedness – or so I've been told by various youngsters – is yet another classic sign that you are fast becoming past it. Sir Josiah Stamp obviously knew this only too well for, while making a speech to the Chicago Club, he expressed concern that he was talking for too long and consequently boring his audience.

'I wouldn't like to be in the position of the parson,' he explained, 'who in the midst of an interminable sermon, suddenly stopped to chide: "You know, I don't mind a bit having you look at your watches to see what time it is, but it really annoys me when you put them up to your ears to see if they are still running."'

LOVELY LONGEVITY

The vicar's message was 'Forgive Your Enemies'.

He asked, 'How many of you have forgiven your enemies?' About half his parishioners held up their hands.

He repeated the question; now about 70 per cent of the congregation answered his query in the affirmative. One more time, he questioned his flock – now all raised their hands, except for one elderly lady.

'Mrs Barrow, are you not willing to forgive your enemies?' the vicar asked, with faint disapproval.

'I don't have any,' she responded proudly.

'Mrs Barrow, that is very uncommon. How old are you?'

'Eighty-seven,' she replied.

'Mrs Barrow, would you please come forward and explain to us all how a person cannot have an enemy in the world.'

The little angelic lady tottered down the aisle and announced, 'It's easy. I just outlived those bitches.'

DEFINITELY PAST IT!

Former US senator Chauncey Depew once found himself seated at dinner next to a young woman with a very low-cut, off-the-shoulder dress. Depew, staring at the young woman's décolletage, leaned over to her and is said to have asked, 'My dear, what is keeping that dress on you?'

'Only your age, Mr Depew,' replied the young woman.

BAD NIGHTGOWN DAY

Searching in the mall for a comfy cotton nightgown, Hannah decided to try her luck in a shop renowned for its sexy lingerie, without much hope of finding something suitable.

However, to her delight, she found the perfect nightdress. Moreover, while waiting in the queue to purchase her selection, she noticed a young woman behind her holding the exact same nightie.

This proved what she had long suspected: despite being in her forties, she had kept up more than adequately with current fashions.

'I see we have the same taste,' she said, somewhat proudly, to the teenager behind her.

'Yes,' the young woman replied. 'I'm getting this for my grandma.'

BAD GOLF DAY

A foursome of golfers hit the course with waning enthusiasm for the game.

'These hills are getting steeper as the years go by,' one moaned.

'These fairways seem to be getting longer too,' said one of the others, with a sigh.

'The sand traps are bigger than I remember them,' moaned the third.

After hearing enough from his friends, the oldest and the wisest of the four of them piped up, 'Just be thankful we're still on the right side of the grass!'

HAIRY GORILLAS

Failing eyesight is always a good test for growing old as Fred Russell, the ageing and almost blind father of theatre impresario Val Parnell, realized to his embarrassment when he went to visit rehearsals of his son's *Sunday Night at the Palladium*.

Having watched Winifred Atwell rehearsing her performance on stage, Russell is said to have turned to his companion and commented on his son's prowess for booking unusual acts, saying, 'He gets some extra-ordinary acts, he does. I've just seen a gorilla playing the piano.'

In actual fact, Ms Atwell was wearing a big fur coat because the theatre was so cold.

LONG MARRIAGES

Getting irritated with your spouse is par for the course, but you really know you're getting on in life when you start telling others just how irritating your partner can be.

Such was the case when the actress Shirley Maclaine asked Samuel Goldwyn's wife, Frances, what it was like being married to the same man for more than thirty-five years.

'It gets worse every day,' replied Mrs Goldwyn. 'Thirty-five years ago, I told Sam to come home and I'd fix him lunch. He's been coming home for lunch every day for thirty-five years!'

AND FOR THE DEFENCE

Charged with armed robbery of a grocery shop in the USA, a forty-seven-year-old man by the name of Dennis Newton decided to dismiss his lawyers and mount his own defence. Assistant district attorney Larry Jones said that Newton was doing quite a fair job of representing himself until the store manager testified that Newton was the robber.

Suddenly, Newton completely lost it and shouted: 'I should have blown your f*****g head off!' before quickly realizing his mistake and adding, 'If I'd been the one that was there.'

The jury subsequently took only a few minutes to convict Newton, who was then handed a thirty-year jail sentence.

HOW BIG?

Two old friends were waiting for a tram. One of them was smoking a cigarette. It started to rain, so the lady reached into her handbag, took out a condom, cut off the tip, slipped it over her ciggie and continued to smoke. It was sort of like a raincoat for her fag.

Her chum saw this and said, 'Hey, that's a good idea! What is it that you put over your cigarette?'

The other lady said, 'It's a condom.'

'A condom? Where do you get those?'

The lady with the cigarette told her friend that you could purchase condoms at the supermarket these days. When the women arrived at their destination, the lady with all the questions went into the local store and asked the shopkeeper if he sold condoms.

He was a little taken aback that this somewhat mature woman was interested in contraceptives, but he asked her, 'What size do you want?'

The lady thought for a minute and then said, 'One that will fit a Camel.'

LEARNING LINES

One day, the director Robert Atkins was rehearsing one of his productions in Regent's Park's open-air theatre when an actress failed to pick up her cue because she had forgotten her lines.

Atkins, noting that she was sitting with her head in her lap, quipped, 'It's no good looking up your entrance, dear – you've missed it.'

HEAVENLY MESSAGES

Two men have been best friends for years, and are a great comfort to each other in their dotage. Suddenly, one of them falls ill. His mate comes to visit him on his deathbed, and they're reminiscing about their long friendship, when the dying man's buddy asks, 'Listen, when you die, do me a favour. I want to know if there's cricket in heaven.'

The sick man replies, 'We've been friends for decades; this I'll do for you.' And then he dies.

A couple of days later, the surviving friend is sleeping when he hears his chum's voice. The voice says, 'I've got some good news and some bad news. The good news is that there's cricket in heaven.'

'What's the bad news?'

'You're bowling on Thursday.'

A RIGHT ROYAL TO-DO

Most men can remember a pretty girl's face quite easily, so British prime minister Benjamin Disraeli must really have been past it when the following occurred.

One day, while talking to a friend, he remarked that he could not recall a particular inn that had been mentioned.

The friend protested: 'You must remember the place, sir. There was a very handsome barmaid there – monstrous fine gal. You must have been in the King's Arms, sir.'

'Perhaps,' responded Disraeli, 'if I had been in *her* arms, I might have remembered it.'

STEP AWAY FROM THE CAR

Jokes are often made about one's driving skills diminishing as one gets older. Whatever the truth of the claim, I think we'd all agree that having one car accident is bad enough, but when you have four in the space of one month – as happened to comedian George Burns – a line really has to be drawn.

After the accidents, Burns decided to employ a driver to take him around, though he still wouldn't admit that his driving was dangerous. He was at pains to point out, only three of those accidents had been his fault!

QUESTION: What is Catholic Alzheimer's Disease?
ANSWER: It's when you forget everything but the guilt.

ROCK STAR LIFE

In January 2003, rock groups KISS and Aerosmith announced that they were going to embark on a world tour together during the forthcoming summer. 'They could call it the Tongue and Lips Tour,' *Salon*'s Amy Reiter suggested.

Sometime later, it was pointed out that both groups had played together more than thirty years earlier.

'On the other hand,' Reiter then joked, 'maybe they should call it the Dentures and Bifocals Tour.'

CHEQUE THIS OUT

There was an ailing gentleman who was a real miser when it came to his money. Just before he died, he said to his wife, 'When I die, I want you to take all my money and put it in the coffin. I want to take my money to the afterlife with me.' And so he got his wife to swear to him, on her mother's grave, that when he passed away, she would put all of his money in his coffin with him.

Well, he eventually died. He was stretched out in the casket, his wife sitting beside him, dressed in black, and her friend sitting next to her. After they'd finished the ceremony, and just before the undertakers got ready to close the coffin, the wife said, 'Wait! Just a moment.'

She had a brown envelope with her, which she placed firmly in the coffin. Then the undertakers locked the coffin and rolled it away.

The wife's friend said, 'I know you were not stupid enough to put all that money in there with your husband.'

The loyal spouse replied, 'Listen, I'm a Christian; I cannot go back on my word. I promised him that I was going to put that money into the casket with him.'

'You mean to tell me you put that money in there?'

'I surely did,' said the wife. 'I got it altogether, put it into my account, and wrote him a cheque. If he can cash it, he can spend it.'

YOU *CAN* BE TOO CAREFUL

After avoiding cashpoint machines for years because of his fears of identity fraud, a man in Germany finally plucked up the courage to use one – and was immediately arrested.

The forty-year-old spent so long checking that the machine was safe – inspecting it for hidden CCTV cameras and even donning a pair of surgical gloves so that he wouldn't leave fingerprints when he entered his PIN – that police picked him up for acting suspiciously.

MARIANNE MOORE'S FLYING CIRCUS

A young man arrived at the home of the American poet Marianne Moore with a stack of books for her to sign. Glancing round the room, the young man admired the bookcases and ornaments, until finally his eyes came to rest on what looked like some sort of medieval contraption hanging by two chains from the door frame.

Marianne Moore was at this time in her seventies, so it seemed impertinent to ask her what it was; nonetheless, the young man plucked up his courage.

'Miss Moore, what is that up there in the doorway?' he said.

Without looking up, she replied, 'Oh, that's my trapeze.'

IT'S A HAT THING

British novelist H. G. Wells is probably best remembered for such books as *The War of the Worlds* (1898) and *The History of Mr Polly* (1910), but what is perhaps less well known about him is that as he grew older, he became increasingly absent-minded ... and eccentric.

For instance, one evening, upon leaving a party he had been attending in Cambridge, he picked up someone else's hat by mistake. On discovering what he had done, however, Wells did not return the item to its rightful owner (whose name was printed inside the brim), but instead wrote him a letter.

'I stole your hat; I like your hat; I shall keep your hat. Whenever I look inside it, I shall think of you and your excellent sherry and of the town of Cambridge. I take off your hat to you.'

HAIR WE GO

In his wonderful tome *Braude's Handbook of Stories for Toastmasters and Speakers*, Jacob Braude relates many wonderful stories and quotes, but one of my favourites is this very silly joke.

'Can you give me a prescription for my hair?' asked the balding patient of his doctor. 'It worries me.'

'Don't worry, old man,' said the specialist, 'it'll all come out all right.'

BEWARE FAIRIES

A couple in their early sixties were celebrating their thirty-fifth wedding anniversary in a secluded picnic area.

Suddenly, a delicate fairy appeared on their tartan rug, saying, 'For being such an exemplary married couple and for being loving to each other for all this time, I will grant you each a wish.'

'Oh, I want to go globe-trotting with my darling husband,' said the woman at once. The fairy waved her magic wand and two reservations for a glamorous round-the-world boat cruise appeared instantly in her hands.

The husband thought for a moment, and then said: 'Well, this is all very romantic, but an opportunity like this will never come again. I'm sorry, my love, but my wish is to have a wife thirty years younger than me.'

The wife and the fairy were deeply disappointed, but a wish is a wish. So the fairy waved her magic wand and the husband became ninety-two years old.

YOU KNOW YOU'RE PAST IT WHEN …

- You begin carrying your senses around in your handbag: glasses, hearing aid, dentures, and so on … – Kurt Strauss

- You're interested in going home before you get to where you're going. – Alan Mainwaring

- You smile at *everyone* because you can't hear a word they're saying.

- Work is a lot less fun – and fun is a lot more work. – Joan Rivers

- Things you buy now won't wear out.

- You like telling stories … over and over and over again.

- Your children are now lying about their age.

- You can't tell the difference between a heart attack and an orgasm.

GOOD OLD GEORGE

When George Clooney was twenty-one years old, he worked as a chauffeur for his late Aunt Rosemary [Clooney] when she was a singer in the 4 Girls 4 with Martha Raye, Kay Starr and Helen O'Connell.

He recalls Raye making him stop the car so she could, as Clooney explained, 'just stick out her leg to take a leak on the side of the road. Aunt Rosemary would say: "Don't turn around, George, or you'll learn too much about the ageing process!"'

THE LIKES OF US

You know you're past it when you're mistaken for a tramp, which is precisely what happened to author Sue Townsend, who wrote the Adrian Mole books and, at the time of this story, also had a play on in the West End of London.

One evening, she was looking through the window of a rather posh restaurant in St Martin's Lane to see if her dinner guests had arrived yet, when she was joined by a tramp carrying several plastic carrier bags and a large, open bottle of sherry, which he proceeded to slop all over the place.

As Sue continued to peer through the restaurant window, she heard the tramp whisper in her ear, 'Ah, it's not for the likes of us …'

WHO ARE YOU TALKING ABOUT?

Three women were sitting side by side in a noisy café one afternoon, reminiscing.

The first lady recalled shopping at the greengrocers in her early married life, and demonstrated with her hands the length and thickness of a cucumber that she could buy for a fraction of today's prices.

The second woman nodded, adding that onions used to be much bigger. She demonstrated the size of the two big onions she used to pick up on her weekly shop.

Then the third lady chipped in with: 'I can't hear a word you're saying, but I remember the guy you're talking about.'

MARITAL MATHS

One day, a frustrated wife told her close friend Jilly her definition of retirement: 'Twice as much husband on half as much pay.'

THE POLITICS OF OLD AGE

Two retired schoolteachers were holidaying with their wives at a villa in the South of France. They were sitting on the patio one warm evening, watching the sun set and sipping cool aperitifs.

The sociology teacher asked his friend, 'Have you read Marx?'

To which his colleague replied, 'Yes and I think it's these damned wicker chairs.'

GARAGE GRASS

Talk about being past it … A woman by the name of Amy Brasher was apparently arrested in San Antonio, Texas on drugs charges after a mechanic reported to police that he had found eighteen packets of marijuana stuffed into the engine of the car that Ms Brasher had brought in to his garage for an oil check.

According to Ms Brasher, she hadn't realized that the mechanic would need to lift the bonnet of the car in order to carry out the job.

DEFINE YOUR AGE

The art historian and novelist Anita Brookner, irritated by the constant speculation about her age which appeared in the press after she had won the Booker Prize for Fiction with *Hotel du Lac* in 1984, wrote to *The Times* on 5 November 1984 to say, 'I am forty-six, and have been for some past time.'

REGRETS, I'VE HAD A FEW

Being past it often involves a great deal of introspection. As we age, we contemplate and review our lives more and more regularly.

On his deathbed, the actor Stanley Holloway (who played Eliza Doolittle's father in the film *My Fair Lady*) was asked whether he had any regrets.

Pausing to think about it, Holloway finally said, 'Yes – the fact that I never got the Kipling cake commercials.'

GOOD NEWS, BAD NEWS

'My grandma told me, "The good news is, after menopause the hair on your legs gets really thin and you don't have to shave any more. Which is great because it means you have more time to work on your new moustache."'   KAREN HUBER

HOME TRUTHS

Late Night show host Conan O'Brien was once asked what his programme's time slot (12.35 a.m.) revealed about his audience.

'It means they're mostly prisoners, pimps, and embezzlers,' Conan replied. 'And a lot of college kids who've just discovered glue sniffing.

'If it's an older person, it means they probably need to take a medication late at night. They come up to me and say, "I put a cream on my ass at 12.34 a.m., and then you come on!"'

OLDER AND MUCH WISER

Sometimes, fun can be had with the younger generation when it comes to being past it. Who among us has not teased and tormented youngsters with our hard-won knowledge and oh so improved capacity for pulling their legs? The following story amply demonstrates the mischievous side of being senior.

One afternoon, a young man, who was an avid golfer, found himself with a couple of hours at his disposal. He quickly came to the conclusion that if he hurried and played very fast, he could squeeze in nine holes on the fairways before he had to attend a business dinner.

Just as he was about to tee off, an old-timer hobbled over and asked if he could accompany the young man as he was golfing alone. Not able to refuse the request, he allowed the old gent to join him.

To his surprise, the man played reasonably well. He didn't hit the ball far, but he pottered along steadily and didn't waste time.

They reached the ninth fairway, and the young man found himself with a tough shot. There was a large oak tree right in front of him, directly between his ball and the green.

He considered how to take the shot for a good long while. Then the young man heard the old man mutter, 'You know, when I was your age, I'd hit the ball right over that tree.'

With that challenge placed before him, the youngster swung hard and hit the ball right smack into the top of the tree trunk, from where it thudded back on the ground, not a metre from where it had originally been.

The old man offered one more comment: 'Of course, when I was your age, that oak tree was only three feet tall.'

SENIOR'S SPEECH

The end of your youth is nigh once you go on and on and on in an increasingly nonsensical manner, much like Sir Laurence Olivier did when he was presented with a special Oscar at the Academy Awards in 1979.

'Mr President and governors of the Academy,' he began, 'committee members, fellows, my very noble and approved good masters, my friends, my fellow students in the great wealth, the great firmament of your nation's generosities, this particular choice may perhaps be found by future generations as a trifle eccentric, but the mere fact of it, the prodigal, pure, human kindness of it, must be seen as a beautiful star in that firmament which shines upon me at this moment, dazzling me a little, but filling me with warmth and the extraordinary elation, the euphoria that happens to so many of us at the first breath of the majestic glow of the new tomorrow.

'From the top of this moment, in the solace, in the kindly emotion that is charging my soul and my heart at this moment, I thank you for this great gift which lends me such a very splendid part in this glorious occasion. Thank you.'

RAIN OR SHINE

Getting hold of the wrong end of the stick is an affliction that increases with age. Worse still is the blasé way in which we nonchalantly reveal our senior selves. Thoughtless statements, thick with miscomprehension, fall as raindrops from our lips – giving all around a good soaking.

One Sunday, for example, a minister was preaching his sermon about the Lord's wisdom in caring for his flock by treating them much like a gardener might treat his plants.

'For instance,' he said, 'our Lord knows which of us fares best in full sunlight and which of us prospers best in the shade. Among us there are roses and heliotrope and geraniums, which flourish in the sunshine. But some of us are more like hellebores, which must be kept in a shady nook.'

After he had finished, a middle-aged woman came up to him, seemingly rejuvenated by what he had taught in church.

'Oh my goodness!' she exclaimed, taking the minister's hand and squeezing it appreciatively. 'That was fantastic. I am so pleased I attended this service.'

The pastor's heart glowed with pride – at long last he had reached out and truly touched another's soul.

'Yes,' the woman continued, 'I am so pleased I came this morning. I never knew before what was wrong with my hellebores.'

> 'There's one more terrifying fact about old people: I'm going to be one soon.'
>
> P. J. O'ROURKE

NINETY-NINE NOT OUT

On being given a huge chocolate birthday cake with ninety-nine candles on top of it, pensioner Edith Anne Drima looked more than a little put out.

'Don't you like it?' asked one of her nurses, concerned.

'It's not a matter of not liking it,' replied Edith sharply. 'If I try to blow all those candles out, I'm going to have a heart attack!'

AGEING DILEMMA

As a guest on *The Tonight Show with Jay Leno* in June 2003, Arnold Schwarzenegger was asked by Leno whether he had had trouble training for his role in *Terminator 3*.

'I know what this is about – the age issue,' Schwarzenegger joked playfully. 'I'm fifty-five years old. It's an awkward age,' he acknowledged. 'You're thirty years too young to date Anna Nicole Smith, but you're thirty years too old to date Demi Moore!'

BOOBIES

The actress Drew Barrymore was once asked during an interview what she thought she might be doing at the ripe old age of fifty.

'Not understanding,' she replied, 'why my boobs are at my ankles!'

MODERN TECHNOLOGY

Yet another sign of impending old age is when technology starts to leave you behind, something that *Private Eye* editor Ian Hislop seems to know all about.

'People tell me that blogs are the future. Oh well, maybe I won't be part of it. I've re-designed the website of *Private Eye* so that when you go on, there's a big message that flashes up, which says: "Go and buy the magazine."'

TONGUE-TWISTERS

You know you're past it when you start getting all your metters lixed up and begin using incorrect words … much like Mrs Levi Zieglerheiter did, according to Kenneth Rose in his book *Superior Person*, published in 1969. Apparently, upon arriving in New York after a stormy ocean crossing, Mrs Zieglerheiter exclaimed, 'At last I am back on terracotta.'

Similarly, according to Nigel Rees in his excellent *Cassell's Dictionary of Anecdotes*, a certain law student, when asked what was necessary for a marriage to be rendered lawful in Scotland, replied: 'For a marriage to be valid in Scotland, it is absolutely necessary that it should be consummated in the presence of two policemen.'

Then there's the story about the dear old grandmother who, on hearing the Beatles' song 'Lucy in the Sky with Diamonds', thought they had sung that the girl with 'kaleidoscope eyes' was actually the girl with 'colitis goes by'! Medical ailments were clearly on her mind.

Finally, there is the story, first told by Kenneth Williams in *The Kenneth Williams Diaries* (1993), about his aged mother, who announced one day, 'Oh! They're opening a lesbian restaurant there!'

Kenneth corrected her: 'It's Lebanese,' but his mother then went on: 'Yes. They're all over the place now, aren't they?'

PREMONITIONS

In 1906, Gertrude Stein had her portrait painted by Pablo Picasso, but it wasn't an easy affair. In fact, the collaboration was a long, arduous one and Stein was asked to sit no fewer than eighty times, after which Picasso declared that he could not 'see' her any more and promptly left for Spain.

Some time later, however, apparently inspired by an exhibit of a particular piece of sculpture at the Louvre in Paris, Picasso completed the portrait and presented it to Gertrude, who immediately complained that she looked nothing like the figure he had portrayed.

'No,' Picasso replied, then added, very unkindly, 'but you will.'

MEDICAL MARVEL

The older we grow, the more there is that can go wrong with us. For some people, getting ill becomes an obsession, almost a full-time job.

Take Victor Meldrew, for instance, from David Renwick's TV show *One Foot in the Grave*, as described by his wife Margaret:

> Victor's one of the few men that suffers from hot flushes. He's had them ever since he stumbled across the details one day in his medical encyclopaedia. Most people have a medical dictionary so that when they get something wrong with them, they can find out

what it is. With Victor, it's the other way round. He looks up a disease and then develops the symptoms to fit it. Treats it more in the way of a Freeman's catalogue, really. Browsing through to see what he can die of next.

WHY WON'T YOU BELIEVE ME?

No one believes seniors ... everyone thinks they are senile.

One day, a couple were celebrating their fiftieth anniversary. They had married as childhood sweethearts and had moved back to their old neighbourhood after they'd retired. Holding hands, they walked back to their old school. The building was locked, but they strolled around the grounds and found the tree trunk on which Trevor had carved 'I love you, Penny'.

On their way back home, a bag of money fell out of an armoured car, practically landing at their feet. Penny quickly picked it up. Not sure what to do with it, they took it home with them. There, Penny counted the money – all seventy thousand pounds of it.

Trevor said instantly, 'We've got to give it back.'

But Penny responded, 'Finders keepers.'

She put the money back in the bag and hid it in their attic.

The next day, two policemen were canvassing the neighbourhood, looking for the money. They knocked on the door. 'Pardon me, but did either of you find a bag that fell out of an armoured car yesterday?' they enquired.

Penny said, 'No.'

Trevor said, 'She's lying. She hid it up in the attic.'

Penny said, 'Don't believe him, he's getting senile.'

The cops turned to Trevor and started to question him. One said: 'Tell us the story from the beginning.'

So Trevor gave a little cough, and began: 'Well, when Penny and I were walking home from school yesterday . . .'

The first policeman turned to his partner and said, 'We're outta here.'

MORE SIGNS YOU'RE PAST IT ...

According to radio presenter Colin Slater, there are a few more signs you're past it:

> You hang your clothes on padded coat hangers; you go supermarket shopping in the evening to pick up marked-down bargains; you save the hearing-aid flyer that falls out of the colour supplement; you try to get electrical gadgets repaired when they go wrong; you store up the free little packets of sugar from cafés; you have worn a knitted swimsuit; when you watch black-and-white films, you spend the whole time pointing at the screen going, 'He's dead ... She's dead ...'; your car stereo is tuned to Radio 2.

I CAN'T HANG ON ANY LONGER, DEAR

The actress Edith Evans was never anything if not direct. Such a quality has even greater liberty with one's increasing years.

During rehearsals for what was proving to be a rather melodramatic play, Evans once said to a much younger fellow actress: 'I'm a very old lady. I may die during one of your pauses.'

YOU KNOW YOU'RE PAST IT WHEN ...

- In a hostage situation, you'd be released first.

- You think of a 'quickie' as grabbing some shut-eye before the traffic lights change.

- Your hair stays on the dressing table at night.

- Someone compliments you on your layered look ... and you're wearing a swimsuit.

- You've reached greener pastures, but you can't get over the fence.

- Your hip sets off a metal detector. – Ross McGuinness

- You light the candles on your birthday cake, and a group of campers form a circle and start singing 'Kumbaya, My Lord'.

- You finally reach the top of the ladder and find it's leaning against the wrong wall.

THE EXCEPTION TO THE RULE

The following is from a seventy-eight-year-old woman who definitely *wasn't* past it when she wrote this letter to her bank manager (who was so impressed that he forwarded it to *The Times*). It gives us all hope that when we grow old, our faculties too might just remain intact.

> Dear Sir,
> I am writing to thank you for bouncing my cheque, with which I endeavoured to pay my plumber last month.
> By my calculations, three 'nanoseconds' must have elapsed between his presenting the cheque and the arrival in my account of the funds needed to honour it. I refer, of course, to

the automatic monthly deposit of my pension, an arrangement which, I admit, has been in place for only eight years.

You are to be commended for seizing that brief window of opportunity, and also for debiting my account £30 by way of penalty for the inconvenience caused to your bank.

My thankfulness springs from the manner in which this incident has caused me to rethink my errant financial ways.

I noticed that whereas I personally attend to your telephone calls and letters, when I try to contact you, I am confronted by the impersonal, overcharging, pre-recorded, faceless entity which your bank has become.

From now on, I, like you, choose only to deal with a flesh-and-blood person.

My mortgage and loan payments will therefore and hereafter no longer be automatic, but will arrive at your bank by cheque, addressed personally and confidentially to an employee at your bank whom you must nominate.

Be aware that it is an offence under the Postal Act for any other person to open such an envelope.

Please find attached an Application Contact Status, which I require your chosen employee to complete.

I am sorry it runs to eight pages, but in order

that I know as much about him or her as your bank knows about me, there is no alternative. Please note that all copies of his or her medical history must be countersigned by a solicitor, and the mandatory details of his/her financial situation (income, debts, assets and liabilities) must be accompanied by documented proof.

In due course, I will issue your employee with a PIN number which he/she must quote in dealings with me. I regret that it cannot be shorter than twenty-eight digits, but, again, I have modelled it on the number of button presses required of me to access my account balance on your phone bank service.

As they say, imitation is the sincerest form of flattery.

Let me level the playing field even further. When you call me, press buttons as follows:

1. To make an appointment to see me.

2. To query a missing payment.

3. To transfer the call to my living room in case I am there.

4. To transfer the call to my bedroom in case I am sleeping.

5. To transfer the call to my toilet in case I am attending to nature.

6. To transfer the call to my mobile phone if I am not at home.

7. To leave a message on my computer. (A password to access my computer is required. A password will be communicated to you at a later date to the Authorized Contact.)

8. To return to the main menu and listen to options 1 through 8.

9. To make a general complaint or enquiry, the contact will then be put on hold, pending the attention of my automated answering service. While this may, on occasion, involve a lengthy wait, uplifting music will play for the duration of the call.

Regrettably, but again following your example, I must also levy an establishment fee to cover the setting up of this new arrangement.

May I wish you a happy, if ever so slightly less prosperous, New Year.

Your Humble Client

ONE FOOT IN THE GRAVE

In the latter part of his life, French composer Daniel Auber was one day attending a funeral service.

'I believe,' he remarked to one of his fellow mourners, 'that this is the last time I'll take part as an amateur.'

BIRTHDAY GREETINGS

The older people get, often the more obstreperous and curmudgeonly they become, as was the case with Sir Thomas Beecham, who, on the occasion of his seventieth birthday, was given a celebratory dinner, during which telegrams and congratulations came in from all over the world – many from the world's greatest musicians and composers.

Even so, according to legend, Beecham was heard to mutter, 'What, nothing from Mozart?'

YOUR CHIPS ARE UP

A man lay frail and gasping on his deathbed. Each breath taken was a valiant struggle to survive. With his last, painful inhalation, however, he suddenly smelled the scent of his favourite chocolate-chip cookies drifting up from the kitchen below … and felt somewhat rejuvenated. He gathered his remaining strength and staggered from his bed.

Leaning heavily against the wall, he gradually made his way from the bedroom and, step by slow step, crawled downstairs on his hands and knees.

The kitchen was now mere metres away. The sunlit room beckoned with its fragrant charm. Were it not for the hacking cough that wrought his body every few paces, he would have thought himself already passed on and in nirvana. For there, spread out upon wire trays on the kitchen surfaces, were literally hundreds of his favourite chocolate-chip biscuits.

Was it heaven? Or was it one final act of heroic love from his devoted wife, seeing to it that he left this world a happy man?

Mustering one great final effort, he crawled towards the table and arranged his withered limbs to sit piously at its foot. His parched lips parted; he could almost taste that familiar cookie dough, seemingly bringing him back to life.

He couldn't stop his wrinkled hand from shaking as it stretched out towards a cookie at the very edge of the table, just within reach. Suddenly, his hand was smacked, hard, with a spatula wielded by his wife.

'Stay out of those,' she said. 'They're for the funeral.'

LOST FOR WORDS

You know you're past it when your mind goes completely blank – but never is this more inopportune than when people are waiting to hear what you have to say, as happened to the American politician John G. Winant.

Once, when asked to make a speech in England, Winant stood in agonized silence for four minutes, before finally whispering: 'The worst mistake I ever made was in getting up in the first place.'

PUZZLED

A man summons his wife and says: 'Look, I've put this cityscape jigsaw puzzle together in six days!'

The wife asks: 'What's so great about you putting a puzzle together in six days?'

'Well, the box says 4–7 years!' replies the man.

SIR WALTER'S BAD MEMORY

Even great writers suffer from occasional lapses of memory, but perhaps none as great as that of Sir Walter Scott, author of titles such as *Ivanhoe* (1819) and *Rob Roy* (1818).

One day in 1819, Sir Walter was given the proofs of his recently completed novel, *The Bride of Lammermoor*. Perusing the proofs, Scott was said to exclaim that he couldn't remember a single character or incident in the entire script.

MISREADINGS

You know you're past it when you can't read words properly ... as the following joke illustrates beautifully.

Two older Jewish ladies, Rebecca and Anne, are at their painting class one morning, when Rebecca says to Anne, 'Wish me good luck. My son finally met a girl and maybe they will get married. But the only thing my son said is that she has herpes. What is herpes?'

Anne replied, 'I don't know, but I have a medical encyclopaedia at home and I will research it for you.'

The next day the ladies meet again, this time at Pilates, and Anne says to her friend, 'Becca, it's OK. You don't have to worry. It's a disease of the gentiles.'

YOU KNOW YOU'RE PAST IT WHEN ...

- Your computer has more memory than you do.

- You realize caution is the only thing you care to exercise.

- You read more and remember less.

- You and your other half wear coordinated outfits.

- Your family discuss you as though you're not in the room.

- Everyone is happy to give you a ride because they don't want you behind the wheel.

- Your body becomes shorter, but your stories become longer.

SWEET DREAMS

In her early career, Germaine Greer was a radical thinker and feminist who placed the issue of gender firmly on the political agenda. At what moment was it that she began grumbling about Christmas cards, senior-style?

'The cards from people are fine,' she says, 'but the ones from organizations really piss me off. I get a card from the firm I once bought a sofabed from – "Merry Christmas, Germaine! From all at Slumbersoft." I don't want Merry Christmas from all at Slumbersoft, thank you very much.'

If you forget where you put your car keys, that's normal. If you don't know what to do with them when you find them, you might be a senior.

KNOBLOCK

The British actor, Sir John Gielgud, was one day dining with a friend of his when he glanced towards the restaurant door.

'Do you see that man just coming in?' said Gielgud. 'Well, he's the biggest bore in London – second only to Edward Knoblock.'

Sadly, Gielgud had forgotten precisely with whom it was he was dining – none other than Edward Knoblock.

SPEEDING SENIORS

A police officer spots a car travelling at just 20 mph. He thinks to himself, 'This tortoise is just as dangerous as the speeding hare!' So he switches on his siren and pulls the driver over.

Approaching the vehicle, he notes that there are four mature ladies inside – two in the front and two in the back – wide-eyed and each of them as white as a sheet.

The driver, clearly bewildered, says to him, 'Officer, I don't understand, I was doing exactly the speed limit! What seems to be the problem?'

'Ma'am,' the officer replies, 'you weren't speeding, but you should know that driving slower than the speed limit can also be a hazard to other road users.'

'Slower than the speed limit? No, sir, I was doing the speed limit exactly... Twenty miles an hour!' the old woman says proudly.

The police officer, trying to stifle a guffaw, explains to her that '20' is the route number, not the speed limit.

A bit shamefaced, the woman smiles and thanks the officer for highlighting her mistake.

'Before I let you go, ma'am,' he says, 'I have to ask – is everyone in this vehicle all right? These women seem awfully quiet and they're looking rather peaky.'

'Oh, they'll be OK in a few moments, sir. We just got off Route 118.'

AT THE WEDDING

At a family wedding, the mother of the bride was determined to keep her eyes bone dry so as not to smudge her delicately applied mascara. She was doing well – until the point in the service when she glanced over at her own mother, who was sitting next to her father.

As she watched the old couple together, her mother reached out to her father, who was at this stage in his life confined to a wheelchair and somewhat incapacitated, and softly stroked his hand. It was such a loving gesture that their daughter found tears running down her cheeks, and she was overcome at last.

After the ceremony, she made her way across the church to where her parents were sitting.

'Mother,' she scolded affectionately, 'it's your fault that I have panda eyes right now. I was holding it together until I saw you reach out for Dad. That just set me off. On this special day, it's wonderful to see the two of you still so much in love.'

Her mother gave an amused snort. 'I'm sorry to ruin your moment, my dear,' she said bluntly, 'but I was just checking to see if he was still alive.'

UNABLE TO DRIVE?

Peter still enjoyed chasing young girls even in his fifties.

When his wife was asked if she minded, she answered, 'Why should I be upset? Dogs chase cars, but they can't drive.'

BEAR SHOOTING

A man in his sixties was having his annual medical check-up and the doctor asked him how he was feeling.

'I've never been better!' the patient boasted. 'I've got a nineteen-year-old bride who's pregnant and having my baby! What do you say to that?'

The doctor considered this for a moment, then said, 'Let me tell you a story. I knew a man who was an avid hunter. He never missed a season. But one day, he went out in a bit of a hurry, and he accidentally grabbed his umbrella instead of his rifle.

'So he was in the woods, and suddenly a grizzly bear appeared right in front of him. He raised up his umbrella, pointed it at the bear and squeezed the handle. And do you know what happened?'

Dumbfounded, the man whispered, 'No.'

The doctor continued, 'The bear dropped dead in front of him.'

'That's impossible!' exclaimed the old man. 'Someone else must have shot that bear.'

'That's kind of what I'm getting at,' replied the doctor.

'Marge, old people don't need excitement. They need to be isolated and studied so it can be determined what nutrients they have that might be extracted for our personal use.'

HOMER SIMPSON'S thoughts on the elderly,
The Simpsons

A WIFE'S REVENGE

'Look at me,' an arrogant gentleman boasted to his guests at his birthday bash. 'I've aged like a fine, old, carefully stored wine.'

'I certainly have to agree with that,' piped up his obviously long-suffering spouse. 'Henry's cork's been stationary for years.'

PERFECT TREATMENT

When you regularly discuss with your friends and acquaintances all your various ailments, and are well informed as to which doctor is best at treating each disease, you know you're well and truly past it – just like the ladies in this next anecdote.

One afternoon, two women, Elsie Nash and Sybil Watts, were sitting in a pretty little café on the high street, discussing Elsie's favourite doctor.

'I don't like your GP,' Sybil commented frankly, sipping her Earl Grey tea, while eyeing Elsie up and down over the rim of her cup. 'He was treating old Mrs White for chronic lung disease for over two years – and eventually she died of a heart attack.'

'So?' said Elsie.

'And he was treating Robert Erskine for kidney disease for over six months and when he finally kicked the bucket, it was of liver disease.'

'But what's your point?' Elsie enquired, taking a large bite out of her carrot cake.

But Sybil simply continued: 'And when he was

treating old Mrs Hunt for pneumonia, she passed away from emphysema.'

'I don't understand,' said Elsie, now putting her cake firmly down on her plate in a gesture of frustration. 'What's wrong with all of that? What are you getting at?'

'Well, when *my* doctor treats you for anything, *that's* what you die of,' replied Sybil, with a triumphant smile.

DAMNED CRICKETS

When the actor and director Mel Brooks was asked by an interviewer what he thought of critics, apparently he misheard the question, for he is said to have replied: 'They're very noisy at night. You can't sleep in the country because of them.'

It was only when the interviewer explained that he had asked about critics not crickets that Brooks corrected the mistake and said: 'Oh, *critics*! What good are they? They can't make music with their hind legs.'

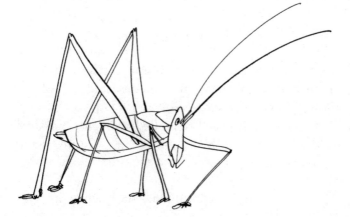

OH, FIDDLESTICKS!

On 9 July 1968, the playwright Alan Bennett recorded the following entry in his diary:

> Spent today auditioning boys at Her Majesty's [for *Forty Years On*]. In the afternoon, when we had been going for about an hour, there was a quavering voice from the Upper Circle. 'Could you tell me when you are going to start, please?' It was an old lady who had come for the matinée of *Fiddler on the Roof* on the wrong day.

THE OLDER MAN

When her name was linked with Sir Robert Mayer, who was 100 years old, Lady Diana Cooper is said to have quipped: 'My dear, when you are my age, you will realize that what you need is the maturer man.'

I AM *NOT* PAST IT

After watching her son Cary Grant on television once, his mother, who was in her nineties, told him off for allowing his hair to go grey.

'It doesn't bother me,' he replied, with good humour.

'Maybe not,' said his mother, 'But it bothers *me*. It makes me seem old.'

YOU KNOW YOU'RE PAST IT WHEN ...

- You look forward to a dull evening at home.

- You don't remember when your wild oats turned to prunes and porridge.

- You finally got your head together – and now your body is disintegrating.

- Getting lucky means you find your car in the parking lot.

- You've got eight pairs of slippers in your wardrobe and only one pair of outdoor shoes.

- You look for the nearest toilet when you go shopping rather than the nearest shop.

- You chip your tooth on a cornflake

- You don't remember being forgetful.

TURN ME ON, TOM!

One afternoon in the Georgia Statehouse, representative Anne Mueller explained to House Speaker Tom Murphy that her microphone had been switched off.

'Mr Speaker, will you please turn me on?' she requested.

'Thirty years ago,' replied Murphy, 'I would have tried!'

GOOD THINGS ABOUT GROWING OLD

On his eightieth birthday, British author Somerset Maugham was making an after-dinner speech at a meal held in his honour at London's Garrick Club.

'There are many virtues in growing old,' he began, before stopping to gaze round the room. The pause continued with Maugham shifting restlessly from foot to foot, rearranging his notes.

Finally, he coughed and continued: 'I'm just trying to think what they are.'

ANY QUESTIONS?

When actress Catherine Zeta-Jones married Michael Douglas, everyone gossiped about the huge age gap.

One morning, when Ms Zeta-Jones was in a department store in Toronto to promote a new fragrance, she was dismayed to find spectators in the crowd beginning to shout out questions.

'Whose diapers do you prefer to change?' one man queried. 'Your baby's or your husband's?'

I'M STILL STANDING ... OR AM I?

Despite having reached seventy years of age, US actor Burt Reynolds was determined to do all his own stunts on the set of the 1998 thriller *Crazy Six*.

'Look, I can do this. I can still fall,' he told the film's producers. 'I just can't get up.'

EZRA POUND

As an old man, the poet Ezra Pound was a virtual recluse, but in *The Oxford Book of American Literary Anecdotes*, editor Donald Hall recounts the following story.

A young poet who was travelling in Italy knocked on Pound's door one day, never expecting the eminent poet to open the door himself. Seconds later, however, Pound appeared in the hallway in his dressing gown and slippers. 'How are you, Mr Pound?' asked the astonished young gentleman. Pound remained silent for quite some time as if pondering the question. Finally, he opened his mouth. 'Senile,' he said.

BABY BOBBIES

The actor and music-hall performer Seymour Hicks definitely knew a thing or two about the signs of being past it when he commented: 'You will recognize, my boy, the first sign of old age: it is when you go out into the streets of London and realize for the first time how young the policemen look.'

FRISKY GRANNY

A mature woman entered a large furniture shop and was greeted by a slip of a salesman. 'Is there something in particular I can show you?' he asked.

'Yes, I want to buy a sexual sofa.'

'You mean a sectional sofa,' he replied.

'Sectional schmectional,' she retorted bitterly. 'All I want is an occasional piece in the sitting room!'

A NEW YOU

The American comedian Bill Cosby obviously knows all about that special era termed one's golden years. Take, for example, the following observation.

'I am having to learn to accept a new me; one who dials a telephone number and, while the phone is ringing, forgets whom he is calling.'

GOOD POINT, MR MORTIMER

It's not pleasant growing old and feeling as if the world has left you behind, but at least John Mortimer has found one positive thing to be said for entering the autumn of one's life.

'Just imagine,' he says, 'what life would be like if you could recite every word of Britney Spears's latest hit.'

A VERY SPECIAL DELIVERY

According to *The Times* newspaper, getting old can be a very confusing time – particularly when your friends send you presents. At least, this was the case for pensioner Fred Harrop.

The paper reported that opera aficionado Harrop was taken aback to receive a book of pornographic images as a birthday gift from chums. In an administrative error, web retailer Amazon.com had sent him *Literate Smut*, containing thirty-five sex snaps, rather than the volume his friends had ordered – *Backstage at the Opera with Cecilia Bartoli.*

Amazon apologized for the mistake, and latterly for the subsequent comment from a company spokesman, who told Harrop's friends: 'If you think Mr Harrop was disappointed, imagine how the guy who got the opera book feels.'

HOME, JAMES!

Nineteenth-century Austrian artist Max Schödel was blatantly past it when he flagged down a taxi in his capital city Vienna one morning.

According to several stories about the incident, the taxi driver, naturally, asked Schödel where he wanted to go.

Schödel had to think for a while before answering, 'Number six.'

That was all he could recall of the address, but he is said to have added, 'Just keep driving and I'll give you the street name when I remember it.'

EGGS

A man was asked by his wife to pick up a bra for her. She told him the correct size and colour, and sent him on his way. By the time he arrived at the shop, however, he had forgotten everything his wife had told him.

A kindly assistant tried to help him out. 'Is she the size of a melon?'

'No, smaller.'

'A grapefruit?'

'No, smaller.'

'An egg?'

'Yes,' shoutd the old man. 'Fried!'

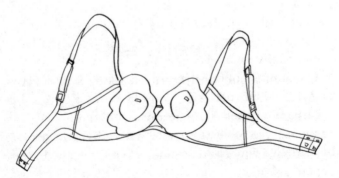

SEX, PLEASE

People often assume that the older you get, the less likely you are to want to make love, but the following story puts pay to all that.

A lady by the name of Millicent was living in an old people's home. One day, she walked into the occupational therapy room and proceeded to parade in front of all the other (mostly male) residents.

Then she clenched her fist and announced to the gathering: 'Anyone who can guess what I have in my closed hand can have sex with me tonight.'

An elderly gentleman with a twinkle in his eye replied, 'A rhinoceros.'

Millicent grinned. 'Close enough,' she said gleefully.

ASPIRIN, DEAR?

Having celebrated their thirtieth wedding anniversary with a slap-up meal at the local restaurant, Barbara thanked Billy for a lovely evening.

'Oh, but it's not finished yet,' said Billy, handing her a small gold box tied with a red silk ribbon.

Barbara opened it excitedly – but there was no anniversary jewellery inside, as she had secretly hoped. Instead, two white pills nestled against the cream tissue paper.

'What are these?' asked Barbara quizzically.

'Paracetamol,' replied Billy.

'But I haven't got a headache.'

'Gotcha!' he exclaimed with a grin.

IF ONLY YOU KNEW

A lady on the wrong side of sixty gets on to a packed bus and stands directly in front of a seated young man. Holding her hand to her chest, she says to the chap, 'If you knew what I have, you would give me your seat.' The man gets up and gives his seat to the lady.

It's a hot day on the bus. The girl sitting next to the woman takes out a fan and starts fanning herself. The lady looks up and says, 'If you knew what I have, you would give me that fan.' The girl, concerned, immediately hands over her fan.

Twenty minutes later, the woman gets up and says to the bus driver, 'Halt! I want to get off here.' The bus driver tells her he has to drop her at the next bus stop; he can't just pull up in the middle of the road. With her hand across her chest, she tells the driver, 'If you knew what I have, you would let me off the bus right here.'

The bus driver applies the brakes and opens the door to let her out. As she's walking off the bus, he asks, 'Madam, what is it you have?'

The wily woman looks at him and nonchalantly replies, 'Chutzpah.'

EIGHTY NOT OUT!

On reaching his eightieth birthday, the actor and raconteur Sir Peter Ustinov quipped, 'I feel I can talk with more authority now, especially when I say, "I don't know."'

FOR THE DEFENCE

As mitigating circumstances go, being slightly senile doesn't spring readily to mind, but the exchange below shows how – if you ever find yourself hauled up in court – being past it might actually be of use.

'You mean to say,' asked the judge incredulously of the defendant, 'that you threw your wife out of the first-floor window through forgetfulness?'

'Yes, sir,' replied the defendant. 'We used to live on the ground floor and I completely forgot we'd moved.'

DISGRUNTLED EMPLOYEES

Misunderstanding something can often be a sign that you're past it, as this incident illustrates.

One day, a woman walked into the Foreign and Commonwealth Office and asked if she could speak to Mr Sexauer. The man to whom she directed her enquiry thought that the gentleman might work in the Home Office, and consequently offered to phone them.

'Do you have a Sexauer over there?' he asked when the telephone was answered.

'Listen,' snapped the woman on the other end of the line, 'we don't even have a ten-minute coffee break any more.'

YOU KNOW YOU'RE PAST IT WHEN ...

- People think you're dead, but are too afraid to ask.

- Your mind not only wanders, but sometimes leaves completely.

- Your childhood toys are now in a museum.

- Everything either dries up or leaks.

- All of your favourite movies are rereleased in colour.

- You buy a compass for the dashboard of your car.

- Your best friend is dating someone half their age – and isn't breaking any laws.

- You feel like the morning after, but did nothing the night before.

LIFE INSURANCE

Often, our spouses realize we're on our last legs long before we do.

One day, John ends up in hospital, having been run over by a ten-ton truck. His best friend Tom goes to see him every day, and every day John tells Tom, 'My wife Katie visits here three times a day. She's so good to me. She brings me sweets and reads to me at the bedside.'

Finally, Tom asks John what Katie is reading to him. 'My life insurance policy, of course!'

GRAVEYARD HUMOUR

There is no surer way to know that you're past it than when you're dead. On his gravestone, the American dramatist Eugene O'Neill had these rather sweet words inscribed:

> EUGENE O'NEILL
> There is something
> To be said
> For being dead

Bibliography

BOOKS

Bennett, Alan, *Poetry in Motion*, BBC Audio Books Limited, London, 1999

Benson, Richard, *Old Git Wit*, Summersdale Publishers Limited, West Sussex, 2006

Braude, Jacob M., *Braude's Handbook of Stories for Toastmasters and Speakers*, Prentice-Hall, Inc., NJ, 1980

Burningham, John, *The Time of Your Life*, Bloomsbury Publishing, London, 2003

Corcoran, Alan, and Green, Joey, *Senior Moments*, Fireside Books, New York, 2002

Enright, D. J., *Play Resumed*, Oxford University Press, Oxford, 1999

Fadiman, Clifton, *The Faber Book of Anecdotes*, Faber and Faber, London, 1985

Friedman, Tom, *1,000 Unforgettable Senior Moments*, Workman Publishing Company, Inc., New York, 2006

Fuller, Edmund (Ed.), *2,500 Anecdotes for All Occasions*, Avenel Books, New York, 1970

Gardner, Hy, *Champagne Before Breakfast*, Henry Holt & Co., New York, 1954

Hall, Donald, *The Oxford Book of American Literary Anecdotes*, Oxford University Press, Oxford, 1981

Hay, Peter, *Broadway Anecdotes*, Oxford University Press, Inc., New York, 1989

Hendrickson, Robert, *British Literary Anecdotes*, Facts on File, New York, 1990

Holder, Judith, *Grumpy Old Women*, BBC Books, London, 2006

Jarman, Colin, *The Guinness Dictionary of Yet More Quotes*, Guinness Publishing Limited, London, 1993

Jarski, Rosemarie, *Grumpy Old Wit*, Ebury Press, London, 2007

Jarski, Rosemarie, *Wrinklies Wit and Wisdom*, Prion, London, 2005

Johnston, Brian, *I Say, I Say, I Say*, Arrow Books, London, 1998

Katz, Eliakim, *Old Age Comes at a Bad Time*, Robson Books, 1988

Marx, Harpo and Barber, Rowland, *Harpo Speaks*, Limelight Editions, New York, 2004

MacHale, Des, *Wit*, Prion, London, 1997

Metcalf, Fred, *The Penguin Dictionary of Modern Humorous Quotations*, Penguin Books Limited, London, 2002

Minkoff, David, *The Ultimate Book of Jewish Jokes*, Robson Books, London, 2005

Petras, Kathryn and Ross, *Age Doesn't Matter Unless You're A Cheese*, Workman Publishing, New York, 2002

Prebble, Stuart, *Grumpy Old Men*, BBC Books, London, 2006

Ratcliff, Susan, *The Oxford Dictionary of Quotations by Subject*, Oxford University Press, Oxford, 2003

Rees, Nigel, *The Cassell Dictionary of Anecdotes*, Cassell & Co., London, 1999

Rees, Nigel, *The Guinness Book of Humorous Anecdotes*, Guinness Publishing Limited, London, 1994

Sampson, Anthony and Sally (Eds), *The Oxford Book of Ages*, Oxford University Press, Oxford, 1988

Sherrin, Ned, *I Wish I'd Said That*, Oxford University Press, Oxford, 2004

Tibballs, Geoff, *The Mammoth Book of Comic Quotes*, Constable & Robinson Limited, London, 2004

Williams, Kenneth, *The Kenneth Williams Diaries*, HarperCollins Limited, London, 1994

Wilson, Richard, *I Don't Believe It!*, Michael O'Mara Books, London, 1996

Watson, Gigi Braynon, *Senior Moments (Did I Do That?)*, XLibris Corporation, USA, 2003

WEBSITES

http://www.4allmemory.com
www.abc.net
www.anecdotage.com
www.ananova.com/news/story
www.basicjokes.com
www.butlerwebs.com
www.c-boom.com/humor2
www.c4vct.com
www.comedy-zone.net
www.davesdaily.com
www.digitaldreamdoor.com
www.dribbleglass.com
www.emmitsburg.net/humor

http://english-jokes.efrr.pl
http://forums.motorcitymoms.com
www.freewit.com/senior-moments.html
www.funbee.com
www.funnyhumor.com
www.geezerweb.com
www.funny-jokes-online.com
www.guy-sports.com
www.gq-magazine.co.uk
www.helium.com
www.homebuilt.org
www.humorbin.com
http://humorvault.tripod.com
www.jamesshuggins.com
www.jokes2go.com
www.jokes.duniya.com
www.jokes-funblog.com
www.jokething.com
http://jokes.maxabout.com
http://www.jokesnjokes.net
www.joke-zone.co.uk/jokes
www.justriddlesandmore.com
http://www.laughy.com
www.mabels.org.uk/old
www.oldpeoplearefunny.com
www.pmcaregivers.com
www.pruneville.com
http://seniorcitizenhumor.blogspot.com
www.seniorsnetwork.co.uk
http://seniors-site.com

www.silvercitizen.com
www.slinkycity.com/funny-news-stories.html
www.suddenlysenior.com/seniorjokebook
www.swapmeetdave.com
www.thedailyquip.com
www.thejokeyard.com
www.unwind.com
http://www.upcheer.com/jokes
www.weirdfunnynews.wordpress.com
http://en.wikipedia.org

NEWSPAPERS AND PERIODICALS

The Daily Telegraph
The Guardian
London News
The Oldie
The Oxford Book of Ages
Reader's Digest
Reuters News Agency
The Times

If you liked this book, you may also enjoy …

The Book of Senior Moments
Shelley Klein
ISBN: 978-1-84317-164-5
£9.99

'Required reading for anyone who has ever suffered a senior moment'
THE OLDIE

If finding your specs is becoming a daily mystery, and family members' names seem to disappear from your mind on a regular basis, you may find that you are suffering from 'senior moments'.

Part guide, part humorous overview, this collection of 'senior moments' is the essential book for anyone interested in … er … whatever it was we were just joking about.

More Senior Moments
Shelley Klein
ISBN: 978-1-84317-256-7
£9.99

The hilarious follow-up to *The Book of Senior Moments*, *More Senior Moments* contains more anecdotes, tips and words of wisdom for those routinely suffering from senior moments.

All Michael O'Mara titles are available by post from:

Bookpost, PO Box 29, Douglas, Isle of Man, IM99 1BQ
Credit cards accepted
Telephone: **01624 677237** Fax: **01624 670923**
Email: **bookshop@enterprise.net**
Internet: **www.bookpost.co.uk**
Free postage and packing in the UK